Reflections on Communication, Education, Scholarship, and Life

Reflections on Communication, Education, Scholarship, and Life

Xin-An Lu

iUniverse, Inc.

New York Lincoln Shanghai

Reflections on Communication, Education, Scholarship, and Life

iUniverse, Inc.

For information address:
iUniverse, Inc.
2021 Pine Lake Road, Suite 100
Lincoln, NE 68512
www.iuniverse.com

ISBN: 0-595-28517-1 (pbk)
ISBN: 0-595-65820-2 (cloth)

Printed in the United States of America

Contents

PART III: Society and Life

PART IV: China

PART I

Communication and Leadership

1

Human-nature Communication

Human-nature communication may be considered as one directional transaction, in which humans bestow their feelings and emotions upon nature. Nature, then, in the human eye, becomes alive. Nature begins to seem anthropomorphic insinuating into every delicate subtlety of the human emotion and idea. Nature in history has been the intimate confidante to many philosophers, writers, and poets.

Religious communication may be considered one form of human-nature communication where God is the medium of Nature. Religious people may disagree since they would consider God as an entity of blood and flesh. Yet, to my knowledge and understanding, no one has been able to communicate with or to be in the "person" of God. Thus I consider God still as one form of Nature. Humannature, or, to some, human-God, communication seems to be purer, more direct, and lucid in that this communication is not burdened with complexities and intricacies of human-human communication.

We can only open ourselves and communicate well by connecting ourselves with an agent and then we may be able to transcend the reality (present customs and conventions) and the noise from the human receiver. Interpersonal communication, in the present world, can hardly promise genuine freedom of expression and even freedom of thought. Too many factors get into the way: ubiquitous stratification of power differences, concern of others' perception of oneself, need to belong to a group, concern about the impact of one's own message on others, protection of one's job and marriage, social taboos, and myriad of other humancreated norms and institutions. Complete freedom in thought and communication may be only attainable in human-nature communication where the human is in complete spontaneous charge. Here, the human will feel a flow of communication—a naturally occurring and self-directing action. It can stay as close to the innermost strings of the heart as the present second to one's breathing; it can go as far as to the most remote time and place in that the human communicator's imagination is blocked by no human-created machinations. This flow of communication represents one that is free; when an object can move with freedom without friction, it promises the highest level of energy and power. This assumption is historically testified. Countless thinkers in history found it imperative to detach themselves from the worldly society and attach themselves to nature, through the medium of which they can incubate and nurture and mature their thinking and the expression of their thinking.

Human-nature communication is pure, not contaminated by human societal conventions or values that may be just expedient products of human imperfections, conditioned indolence, and even morbid intentions. In human-nature communication, the human can design and build her own model according to her own aspiring ideals. The form follows the idea instead of the other way around, as happens all the time in human-human communication. The human can always revise the model if she finds it going even slightly away from her ideals. When communication is free from conventional customs and values, the human begins to feel as if responding to the ultimate righteousness instead of to the mundane righteousness conditioned by societal artifices. Human-human communication can never sprint; it can only hobble at its best, in that, for one thing, human-human communication has to heed stipulated norms, forms, styles, specifications, jargons, validity as understood by hair-splitting pedants...Our society is far from being a product of our ideals. Our society is still a product of our very imperfect interactions. Our actions and interactions more often than not are not directed by our ideals and consciousness, but by mere expediencies and nonchalance. Consequently, we unconsciously let our externally conditioned actions and interactions guide us and what we produce are reactions subsequent to these actions and reactions. This is too bad, because what we are supposed to do is make building blocks for our ideal castle and put them in the desired structure. This is perhaps why some say every individual is good. When individuals come together, they become bad because they then become directed by their interactions instead of by their conscious ideals. This is also why communication can become very frustrating and even destructive of the human-human bond if we forget what we are communicating for and let communication become something for its own sake. A careful reflection and analysis of human norms and artifices is likely to reveal that the bulk of human cultural and societal contrivances are but to make human-human interactions controllable or expedient for those in power rather than to facilitate the birth of genuine human ideas and ideals.

We should never let communication be representative of the communicator. Communication is only the bridge or the vehicle through which the communicator tries to arrive at the home of his ideals. That is, we should never judge a person by how he communicates, but by what he communicates; not by the medium of communication, but by the message of communication.

Too frequently in our life, we forget our purpose and our task. Then we begin to judge and get judged by the way we communicate rather than by what we communicate. This human folly may be epitomized in scholarly publications, the bulk of which serve no other purpose than get someone to the next rung along the spectrum of artificial denominations and get some more pages (fraught with coherent insignificances), bounded in a nice-looking volume.

Human-nature communication is desirable and welcome. It is largely free from the danger involved in human-human communication. Even intra-personal communication is less desirable than human-nature communication. Intra-personal communication is still one between two people—the true self and the social self. The social self is a hard person to communicate with because its face is hard to decipher and its intention hard to interpret. Human-nature communication is one with the true self via the facilitative medium of nature, neither of which (nature and the true self) is contaminated by social contrivances. More importantly, nature responds and teaches the communicator in a purely honest and inspiring way and in a slow yet melodiously persuasive way.

Human-nature communication often is a spiritual journey toward the dreamland, a promise only by the ultimate and unquenchable human aspirations. It is no exaggeration to claim that many monks and nuns actually feel less lonely and more inspired with time. Judged by conventional thinking, they should be more and more lonely with time. (Yet conventional thinking to me more confuses than explains.) Our understanding of "evidence" has long led us to confuse psychological conditions with physical realities; the feeling of leisure and busyness, for instance, is by no means a physical reality, but purely a psychological condition. The fact that the majority of our fellows feel they are very busy does not indicate that we are doing and producing more, but that our society is debilitating and emaciating.

Human-nature communication is a nurturing process, a process of growth. In this communication, enough time is allowed for dreams to be birthed, clarified, expressed, and reified. It is only not until you have your aspirations and purposes clarified and reified, can you find clear means to realize them. The image of purpose in human-human communication has long become blurred. We spend the bulk of our waking hours to do things simply because these things are ubiquitous instituted human practices. A careful reflection of the purpose of these things will not uplift you to the sunlight mount of hope and energy, but will quickly plummet you to the abysm of confusion and pessimism.

Human-nature communication teaches us what we should teach in our communication courses. What matters are not mechanical skills but lasting and heartfelt values, beliefs, ideals, and dreams. Mechanical skills in communication, if not armed with beliefs, can never escape getting finally killed by conventional and powerful communication practices everywhere around us. I believe "skilled" communicators, often represented by great leaders like Martin Luther King, Jr., are not people with skills but people with beliefs and aspirations. For effective communication, we should have an agent or buffer between the speaker and the listener. The agent or buffer is not skills but beliefs. Skills can never help you transcend "bad" responses in communication that may immediately abort the attempt for better communication. It is beliefs that transcend, edify, and transform. Real learning is not a matter of dealing but one of transcending and finally being. All commercial textbooks for the basic communication courses are largely failures (achieved with multi-hundred-page pomposity and vacuity) if the purpose of the course is to transform and edify the learners' communication beliefs and practices.

2

Nervousness and Stage Fright

Nervousness is but natural, yet we sometimes need to learn to act unnaturally to be up to great occasions. When we first learn to play the violin, being clumsy is natural. We have to be unnatural with the fingers for a long time so that we can eventually master the sublime naturalness of virtuosity. Fear is natural, but people grow by learning to overcome fears. Also, before you can do something, you have to be that. For example, before you can be the president of the nation, you probably have to speak, act, and be like the president. Later on in our life we will realize that most fear and nervousness we experience is but self-imposed. People in this world around us are too busy to care about nervousness from you.

One other thing that helps overcome fear and nervousness is our psychological relationship with the external and internal world. I found that if I detach myself from the external world, or from "what is," and attach myself to my internal world, or to the world of "what could be," I begin to feel a communion with my message to communicate. My heart and body are with the message instead of with the audience. Communion with the internal message of my dreams, plans, and aspirations will uplift me with energy, poise, and presence of mind. Communion with the audience just injects into the heart fear and self-consciousness. Good public speaking should be an externalization of some fiery passion and plan. If it is just a wish to appear nice, to successfully perform some task, or to please some people, no excellence would be achieved in public speaking.

3

Purpose of Rhetoric and Language

The purpose of rhetoric is to clarify and unify by seeking the truth. For this purpose, language should be as direct, simple and unembellished as possible.

My topic on the purpose of rhetoric apparently sounds too broad to be one for a student paper, but I believe the study of purpose should be the first step for all sciences. A unified purpose defines, thus clarifies, thus unites, and thus directs. "We define first and then see" (Oliver, 1961, p. 31). One of the biggest problems with modern humanity sciences is that they produce interminable controversies because they use too many definitions. Too many definitions absolutely do not define. It seems that, in our time, the more you study, the less you know. The end product of scholarship can easily become agnosticism, which is only made to appear scholarly through arcane language and narrowed logic. All this is a clear symptom of lack of a primal, unified purpose. This lack plagues us with a plethora of definitions. A plethora of definitions only produces a great mass of controversies. A great mass of controversies only confuses instead of edifies, making it impossible for us to "poetically dwell on the earth" (Heidegger, 1977, p. 316).

Therefore, before studying rhetoric, let's ask this question: What purpose should rhetoric serve so that it clarifies and leads instead of confuses and misleads? One way to endeavor for an answer to this question is by examining what purposes are implied behind different definitions of rhetoric.

Definition one:[1] Rhetoric is the practice of (effective) oratory. The purpose of rhetoric implied by this definition is contained in the purpose of oratory. To Cicero (1990), effective oratory should be able to teach, to move and to delight. To delight itself is an end, but what needs a further answer is the question of

---

1. The six definitions to rhetoric used in this article are taken from: Bizzell, P. & Herzberg, B. (Eds.). (1990). The rhetorical tradition: Readings from classical times to the present. Boston: Bedford/St. Martin's.

teaching what, and moving the audience towards what. To Aristotle (1990), oratory is "the faculty of observing in any given case the available means of persuasion" (p. 153). Although some rhetoricians assign a purpose to oratory (e.g., Aristotle and Augustine), this definition itself does not imply a subject matter for rhetoric or a purpose beyond persuasion, which can be highly situational.

Definition two: Rhetoric is the use of language, written or spoken, to inform or persuade. According to this definition, language apparently serves as the means or the tool. Thus language can be formed, deformed or embellished in whatever a way that can serve the purpose of informing and persuading. Thus language can be used not only to reveal but also to conceal information so that it informs in the way desired by the informer, speaker, or rhetor. Thus, to persuade, language can be manipulated in such a way that it plays best with the audience's emotions and logic, which more often than not are conditioned by the audience's current social situation. This definition obviously makes rhetoric too much relative and situational. It all depends on the audience and the situation to determine what and how to inform and persuade, so that rhetoric can possibly influence. All this sounds much like Gorgias. To Gorgias, there is no absolute truth; our knowledge is situational and provisional (Bizzell & Herzberg, 1990).

Definition three: Rhetoric is the study of the persuasive effects of language. Language in this case is put under a similar fate as it is in definition two. Because of the imbalanced emphasis on different features of language, language will consequently look rather physically deformed, with one part of its body (persuasive characteristics) strengthened and the development of the rest (e.g., descriptive features) ignored. Furthermore, when language is used solely for persuasion, relativism is ready to appear. Controversies will follow up quickly.

Definition four: Rhetoric is the study of the relation between language and knowledge. The question necessitated by this definition is: Is our knowledge conditioned or formed by our way of using language (The fact that some cultures nurture more philosophers than others is perhaps due to their language structures), or the way we use our language is conditioned by our pursuits of knowledge. Gorgias and Nietzsche seem to support the former idea. Gorgias and Nietzsche contend that language conveys only opinions, which constitute our sole knowledge (Bizzell & Herzberg, 1990). Thus our knowledge is conditioned by our language, which our society and culture arbitrarily determine. The explicit connotation in this definition again is agnosticism, which produces but endless controversies.

Definition five: Rhetoric is the classification and use of tropes and figures. This definition subjects language to the status of the monkey in a circus. Language is manipulated so that it can be played with, perhaps to amuse. According to Nietzsche, tropes are the most artistic form of rhetoric. Rhetoric, because of its dependence on language, is actually all figuration. Truth, obtained through rhetoric, is merely a social arrangement dictated by a certain power (Nietzsche, in Bizzell & Herzberg, 1990). Under this definition of rhetoric, agnosticism is again ready to surface.

Definition six: Rhetoric is the use of empty promises and half-truths as a form of propaganda. This one sounds more blatant in its ulterior or even subversive motives. No wonder, few of the great ancient theorists on rhetoric explicitly adopt this definition.

I believe, as claimed by Bizzell and Herzberg (1990), that the above list of definitions is far from exhaustive. Every definition within itself also produces complications and controversies, because of their nature of relativism. If scholars are already lost in the clouds of a wealth of definitions and their potential complications, how can scholars within this discipline argue with each other (They can only argue past each other), so that they can cooperatively build up the discipline; so that the study in the discipline clarifies, inspires and leads, instead of confuses, overwhelms and discourages. I believe the phenomenon of departmentalization comes from a sense of hopelessness and resignation, from the realization that a direction in a certain discipline can hardly be achieved without a pinpointed concentration on a pinpointed tiny spot within this discipline. The necessary result of departmentalization is an explosion of directions that are no direction at all, and a lack of unity in crucial human matters. All this leads to our disintegration socially, morally and scientifically. Because of modern developments in sciences, we are plagued with a "multitude of the eloquent" (Augustine, 1990, p. 387), who subject us to interminable controversies in every respect. Because of this "multitude of the eloquent," universities are from becoming the center of order and light. For rhetoric to serve humankind the best, it should be blessed, instead, with a "multitude of the wise" (Augustine, 1990, p. 387).

What is the wise? The wise is the messenger of the truth. The purpose of rhetoric is to seek, clarify and find the truth. In this sense I tend to stand with Lao-tzu and Plato. Then what is the truth? My rather pessimistic view of our world enables me with temerity enough to venture for a definition of truth: the primal, final, and absolute human wish that unifies, engages and offers the greatest joy possible for the greatest number of people possible. To conventional logic and wisdom, this definition of truth sounds (no, is) stupid enough because it is utopian. It is not utopian to me because I am counting on rhetoric, the greatest tool humankind has ever invented. Rhetoric is the linguistic bridge whereby we know ourselves so that we, blessed with the truth, are able to fulfill ourselves.

Whether we can count on rhetoric to fulfill its assigned noble mission, depends upon how we use the servant of rhetoric, language. In many cultures, language is used (or abused, as indicated in the above-mentioned definitions of rhetoric) not only to express but also to cover up what is really in people's minds. What is worse, the latter function assigned to language frequently outweighs the former. If language is used to cover up so that the power group can maintain a certain social order or structure, language only confuses and complicates. In this case, the better the speaker speaks, the more he or she actually confuses and complicates. What is more vicious, some speakers can speak so well that the public accepts their assumptions and arguments as facts or as the only way our life has to go. This is perhaps why Taoists contend, "In much talk there is great weariness. It is best to keep silent" (cited in Oliver, 1961, p. 28). Lao-tzu's principal teaching is that we "should be in harmony with, not in rebellion against, the fundamental laws of the universe" (cited in Oliver, 1961, pp. 28-29). I am not quite sure about what Lao-tzu exactly means by his "fundamental laws of the universe." I am not certain either about what Plato exactly means by his "absolute truth." What is important is that they both argue for a final purpose that rhetoric should serve. Concerning the use of language and truth, Gorgias takes rather a resigned attitude. He argues, "We achieve confidence in our own wisdom only through deception, not knowing that we do not know," and that language in use creates and changes the opinions that are our only available knowledge (Bizzell & Herzberg, 1990, p. 38). Obviously, when language usurps the crown of rhetoric, the only result is agnosticism. When language usurps the crown of rhetoric, the eloquent takes away the power which should belong to the truth. Thus, criminals can roam our streets leisurely because of the eloquent lawyers they can afford to hire.

In our education, we are facing rather a sad situation concerning the question of language and truth. The educated may not be those who get closer to truth (e.g., by becoming more virtuous), but are frequently those who can speak voluminously (e.g., by publishing a lot) and sound good. Someone told me that the educated are people who should be able to speak eloquently without saying much. To me, this definition of the educated is more illuminating than cynical. It illuminates a lack of purpose.

My philosophy for rhetoric is: Language serves rhetoric; rhetoric serves truth. If rhetoric does not serve truth, do away with it; if language does not serve rhetoric, do away with it (can we?). This is why "[t]he principle of Tao is spontaneity"

(Oliver, 1961, p. 31). The use of language, which depends on strict and long training and careful manipulation, can easily destroy spontaneity. When we are endeavoring for the word, the thought is already gone miles away. Yet, without language, what is the medium through which truth may possibly emerge? Perhaps I should qualify my argument concerning rhetoric and language. Without language, truth cannot emerge; when language rules, truth disappears. Rhetoric and language should not be the privileged art of the educated and powerful. Armed with rhetoric, rhetoricians and linguists should help the populace to express themselves. We find real rhetoric not in the beauty of speeches. We find it in how truly it helps to bring out and represents the minds of the populace. For this purpose, language should be as simple and direct as possible. Embellished language not only covers up, complicates and distorts, but more importantly it repels the populace, whereby truth can hope to emerge.

When language cannot express the truth (What is truly in people's minds), it becomes more embellished and manipulated to fulfill other functions than expression. What happened during the period of imperial Rome can be an example. One of the major reasons why the rhetors during this period are Sophists, was that they, who were politically restrained, could not use language to express, but to entertain. Language that does not express becomes embellished. Embellished language does not express.

Rhetoric, for the unified purpose of seeking truth, needs language, but should never become dependent upon language. When rhetoric becomes the art of language, it defeats its noble purpose.

References:

Aristotle. (1990). Rhetoric, Book I (W. Rhys Roberts, Trans.). In Bizzell, P. & Herzberg, B. (Eds.), The rhetorical tradition: Readings from classical times to the present (pp. 151-94). Boston: Bedford/St. Martin's.

Augustine. (1990). On Christian Doctrine, Book IV (T. Sullivan, Trans.). In Bizzell, P. & Herzberg, B. (Eds.), The rhetorical tradition: Readings from classical times to the present (pp. 386-422). Boston: Bedford/St. Martin's.

Bizzell, P. & Herzberg, B. (Eds.). (1990). The rhetorical tradition: Readings from classical times to the present. Boston: Bedford/St. Martin's.

Cicero, M. T. (1990). Of oratory, Books I-III (E. W. Sutton & H. Rackham, Trans.). In Bizzell, P. & Herzberg, B. (Eds.), The rhetorical tradition: Readings from classical times to the present (pp. 200-250). Boston: Bedford/St. Martin's.

Heidegger, M. (1977). The question concerning technology. In D. F. Krell (Ed.), Martin Heidegger: Basic writings (pp. 287-317). New York: Harper & Row.

Oliver, R. T. (1961). The rhetorical implications of Taoism. Quarterly Journal of Speech, 47, 27-35.

4

The Web and a Sense of Home for Overseas Chinese Students in America

Humans always have a need for a sense of community, however small it may be. To achieve this community, we depend on communication. In very ancient times, people used fire and smoke on a high spot to signal the coming of enemy to the rest of their community. They could achieve basic communication through this primitive means simply because their community was geographically very small. Later on when people developed more advanced transportation devices, they acquired more mobility, and their community kept expanding. The need for sophisticated and long-range communication increased tremendously. The scope of human community and communication has, up to now, expanded to the global level. This can be both a fortune and misfortune, depending on whether adequate means are available for émigrés to maintain a sense of home when they are away from their indigenous culture.

When international students come to study in the United States, they are usually dispersed throughout the whole area of this country, and immersed in the sea of American students and teachers. They no longer have a community of their own race and culture. Their sense of community is very much diluted. They can become extremely homesick, especially during the initial period of their arrival. In this essay I will talk about how several important websites provide a democratic public forum, a sense of community, and a possibility to feel the motherland for the sparsely dispersed Chinese students studying in the United States.

One website which great numbers of Chinese students access every Friday (New issues come out on Fridays) is China News Digest (CND, available at: http://cnd.cnd.org). It has led to an interesting phenomenon in Faner Hall at Southern Illinois University at Carbondale which boasts a population of about 1000 Chinese students. Here every Friday, I can see many Chinese students reading, on the Web, the same magazine in their own language. I have talked with and interviewed some Chinese students for their comments on the Chinese websites I will address in this paper. Miss Wang Xiaoyan[1] said, "I can delay every assigned reading but I won't do that to China New Digest. On China News Digest I hear many dissenting voices which I could not hope to hear when I was back in China." One of the most important reasons why many Chinese students like China News Digest is its democratic editorship and its pro-democracy tendency. Its news reporting, for example, is very much balanced. Readers not only can see good news about China which abounds in traditional Chinese mass media, but also negative news, which readers do not usually see on mass media back in China.

China News Digest can achieve this not only because it is sponsored in a land free from control by the Chinese government, but also because the form of computer-mediated communication itself offers a greater possibility for free expression. Kedzie (1997) argues that computer interconnectivity is not only the greatest predictor of, but also contributes vastly to, democracy. Computer-mediated communication (CMC), especially the World Wide Web (WWW), always seems to promise a greater possibility for quicker and more frank reflections and more perspectives of the outside world.

What makes CMC particularly powerful as a contributor to democratization is its interactive many-to-many pattern of communication. Telephone is generally one-to-one or one-to-several. TV is one-to-many. Newspaper is one-to-many. The communication pattern of the Internet is exactly what was in the minds of the designers of ARPANET, the predecessor of Internet. Destruction of one node in the web does not damage the web as a whole. Messages flow in so many directions through so many nodes that they broadcast in the truest sense. CMC makes the "democratic message become duplicable, adaptable, and redirectable, almost effortlessly. The medium also provides for accountability and permanence of messages. The messages themselves are tractable to analysis and verification. These are all capabilities that play away from a dictator's iron hand" (Kedzie, 1997, p. 226).

Many of these characteristics are reflected through the website of China News Digest. In almost every issue of this electronic magazine, I can find dissenting and conflicting viewpoints on Chinese politics, history, economy, Tibet issues and democracy. Most of the articles published in this electronic magazine are written

---

1. For confidentiality, the names of the Chinese students that I use in this paper are not real unless otherwise indicated.

by students and scholars in the United States. All this is almost impossible in mass media in mainland China. Two supplemental issues[2] of China News Digest carried the unabridged scripts of its extensive interview with Wei Jingsheng, perhaps the most famous dissenter in China. There was elaborate description of the inhuman treatment he received during his imprisonment. On the other hand, I also see many views on China News Digest which are in strong support of those practices by the Chinese government. I believe if Chinese government gets to read this electronic magazine, it will get a true flavor of freedom in speech. It will consequently realize that freedom in speech is nothing as fearful as the government imagines, and that freedom of speech will not lead to totally one-sided criticism against the government.

Another factor that makes China News Digest a very democratic magazine is the fact that the sponsors of this magazine are all volunteers, composed of Chinese students and scholars in the United States. They are not much influenced either by politics or by economics. That is perhaps why the style of their editorship is very democratic. After its extensive interview with Wei Jingsheng, China News Digest published a series[3] of readers' responses to this interview. Some responses are very harsh against this magazine. One reads, "I can't understand why China News Digest spends so much time interviewing and publishing a jerk like Wei Jingsheng. It seems that China News Digest could use its volunteers' time in a more useful way." Another reads, "China News Digest does not seem to be free from bias at all" (See Issues #357 and #358). Despite all the conflicts in viewpoints, I can see much frankness, honesty, and sincerity in many contributors who collaborate in their efforts for solutions to China's myriad of problems. This is perhaps the real power of the democratic forum provided by Web forums. Mr. Zhang Wenxuan said, "When reading the conflicting views on China News Digest, I feel we come from one big family. Although we argue and disagree, we are trying to solve our own problems."

Very interestingly, I also found on China News Digest an article representing Chinese farmers' voice. This is rare. Chinese farmers are literally on the lowest rung of the social ladder in China. They are in greater difficulty than anybody else to get their voice heard through mass media in China. But through a website so far away from their own homeland, they achieved this (probably through a relative or friend). The power of CMC shows itself again in this case.

---

2.   China News Digest Supplemental Issues ZK # 140 (1, 2).
3.   See China News Digest Issues #357 and #358.

Besides being a good public forum for overseas Chinese students and scholars, China News Digest promptly provides them with updated news about China. Carbondale, Illinois is a small place, different from places like San Francisco and Los Angeles. It is not easy at all for Chinese students and scholars here to get magazines and newspapers in their own language. Furthermore, I do not think the Chinese students will spend their own hard-earned money on subscriptions to newspapers and magazines. Thus the news provided by China News Digest is greatly valued. Perhaps to the majority of the Chinese students here at Southern Illinois University at Carbondale, CND news provides one of the very few means to keep in touch with the most recent developments in China. Miss Zhou Xiao-qing, a doctoral student in chemistry, said, "Every Friday, when I sit down to read the news, I feel I'm back in Beijing again." I can see joy and gratitude in her eyes.

China News Digest also carries articles that try to offer solutions to practical daily problems that Chinese students and scholars face in their U.S. study, life, and work. In this sense CND is a free consultation service for these people. They find a friendly "chat room" in those articles, which describe the joys and difficulties of Chinese students and scholars in the United States. This makes them feel that they are not alone in many difficult situations. All this can offer great help in overcoming loneliness and depression. I also hope those who are back in China and plan to study in the United States are reading these articles. This will help them understand much better the life of studying in America and thus help them make a more advised decision before they embark on the long process of preparing to study in the United States.

Homesickness is perhaps the biggest disease Chinese students face when they first come to America. Email, of course, plays a great role in this respect. Yet many websites or links also do a great job in helping relieve the homesickness of Chinese students. Although Chinese students here are not physically together with their homeland, "[t]he substitution of electronic data for physical association easily leads to the substitution of" their former "form of sensually being-with-others" for a new one (Deetz, 1990, p. 53). One such homesickness-curing website is called Xin Yu Si (the New Literature Thread, available at http://www.xys.org). This site contains a vast world of Chinese magazines, newspapers, books, pictures, paintings…. Simply sitting before the monitor, the Chinese students can access almost whatever Chinese readings their imagination can conjure up. Reading about their own culture in their own language is an enormous alleviation for those homesick overseas students. Miss Lin Hua told me that whenever she got homesick about China, the thing that she will most likely do is read Chinese on the Internet, including the site called the New Literature Thread. She specifically emphasized the scenery pictures of China, which enable her to have "virtual" travels of her motherland, or even her hometown. What makes the website of "the New Literature Thread" more interesting and valuable is its rare collection of photos and novels. Some of these photos and novels are banned in mainland China. It is really wonderful to be able to access something which not only relieves your homesickness, but also gives you information not obtainable at home. For example, photos of the Tiananmen Square pro-democracy movement in 1989 constitute a great historical collection. Also accessible through the New Literature Thread are some famous classical Chinese novels still banned in China.

Access to Chinese songs and traditional music is another wonderful thing the World Wide Web can offer to overseas Chinese students in the United States when they miss home. The newly established "Chinese Yahoo" (or SinoYahoo, or Sohoo, available at http://www.sohoo.com.cn) offers such sites. Living in the United States, I feel nothing reminds me better of home than does the music of my homeland. Sohoo has a large collection of Chinese songs and folk music, from popular singers of Taiwan and Hong Kong to those of the mainland, from songs of the 60s to those of present, from folk music to rock-n'-roll. I seem to be able to relive every period of my past via listening on the Web to the songs and music of that period, a real luxury for a person living far away from his/her homeland. Mr. Wang Cheng said, "When I put on those head-phones and listen to those songs and music so familiar, everything American retreats into the forgotten background—people speaking English, English on the walls,…. The music and songs, through their audio effect of the melody and their Chinese lyrics, create for me an encompassing world of home culture. I'm so much immersed in the world produced by the songs that, at such moments, I feel completely at home typing on my own computer."

Reading Internet publications can be considered as a unidirectional computer-mediated communication. The dynamics appears much weaker than that of synchronous CMC, like Internet Relay Chat (IRC). Yet I feel more inclined to engage in reading Web publications. These publications represent, at the reader's fingertips, a constellation of the various and the many. Whatever my wish and mood at the moment, it seems that I can always find something on the Web to suit them. On the Web, the past, the present, and even the future converge; the near and the far get united. Everything is "packaged" into a wonder box which is put at my fingertips. It is an idea of "have this little wonder box, and you have everything." "[P]erhaps one thing we can learn from the Net is that there is no closure" (Argyle, 1996, p. 140). The Net is a free and open space. The bane of geographical dislocation and dispersion is transformed by the Net. Accordingly our concept of *home* is also changed. Home becomes more of a concept of access to information than one of physical location. Where you no longer matters much. What you think and feel begins to matter more. Perhaps in the future, the Net will bless us with a sense of home regardless of our physical location.

References

Argyle, K. (1996). Life after death. In R. Shields (Ed.), <u>Cultures of Internet: Virtual spaces, real history, living bodies</u> (pp. 133-142). Thousand Oaks, CA: Sage Publications Inc.

Deetz, S. (1990). Representation of interests and the new communication technologies: Issues in democracy and policy. In M. J. Medhurst, A. Gonzalez & T. R. Peterson (Eds.), <u>Communication and the culture of technology</u> (pp. 43-62). Pullman, WA: Washington State University Press.

Kedzie, C. R. (1997). A brave new world or a new world order? In S. Kiesler, <u>Culture of the Internet</u> (pp. 209-232). Mahwah, NJ: Lawrence Erlbaum Associates, Publishers.

5

The Study of Attitude and Human Communication

The study of attitude is not only a very important area in social psychology, but also has much to offer to the research and betterment of human communication. Human actions, including communicative actions, do not always grow out of reason and logic. More frequently human actions perhaps are determined by a combination of factors like mood, emotions, personal perception, and interpersonal interactions. All these factors may be distilled into and manifested in the form of personal attitude. Thus a better understanding of attitude will surely offer us a firmer grasp on the handle of our communicative behaviors. Of course some may argue that change in behaviors can also lead to change in attitude. This may be true. Yet this argument does not in any way detract from the importance of attitude as a major predictor of human communicative actions.

Research has demonstrated that attitude change can come from cognitive dissonance. Cognitive dissonance produces psychological discomfort which, in turn, motivates an attitude change. The greater the cognitive dissonance, the greater the psychological discomfort, and, hence, the greater the attitude change. The degree of cognitive dissonance is determined by the difficulty level in accounting for the dissonant behavior. The higher the difficulty level, the greater the cognitive dissonance, and the greater the possibility for attitude change. When a dissonant behavior (one against privately held beliefs) happens, we tend to explain away this behavior in order to maintain psychological consistency. Coercion provides us with a handy answer to explain away such dissonance. Therefore, coercion decreases the difficulty level in explaining a dissonant behavior, and thus decreases cognitive dissonance, and thus decreases the possibility for attitude change.

One article from *New York Times* talks about the effect from people's positive attitude toward George Washington. This positive attitude influenced many artists so that they transform Washington into portrayals of different role models like the military strategist, the successful farmer, and the dedicated family member. This shows that a certain attitude can nurture a certain action. A second article from *Written Communication* discovered that the ability of written persuasion to change readers' attitude is not only affected by text characteristics but also by reader characteristics. A third article from *Human Communication Research* found that people have implicit persuasion theories. People's implicit persuasion theories determine the acceptability and topical relevance of the persuasion. Thus persuasion is not merely a matter of the persuader, but, perhaps more importantly, a matter of those to be persuaded. A fourth article from *Journal of Communication* discovered that people's attitude is more affected by their local culture or co-culture which is formed by people's communications with those nearby. This shows the importance of "local logic or knowledge" in persuasion.

The above research results and reflections on attitude remind me of a major weakness in many introductory courses of human communication. The textbooks of many such courses devote the bulk of their pages to the explanation of communication theories, concepts, and skills or techniques. This explanation will mainly broaden the scope of the students' *knowledge*. Knowledge alone does not promise well a change in behavior. Attitude must be given greater attention. However, commercial textbooks do not seem to be able to stir any strings in the students' heart. How can we expect these books to affect students' attitude.

Traditional psychologists probably give importance to behaviors than to anything else not only because they believe that only behaviors are observable, but also because behavioral change is probably the ultimate end of all psychological research, persuasion, and education. This is especially true to communication education. To be blunt, a communication education course is very much a failure without producing positive behavioral changes in the students.

Thus I am suspecting the wisdom of many introductory (and even advanced) communication courses when they place their major efforts on explanation of knowledge components such as definitions, concepts, and techniques. Yet, as I argued in previous paragraphs and as research results on attitude have demonstrated, our actions are more influenced by our attitudes than by our logical knowledge (Too often, we do what we *know* is bad). Knowledge does not automatically translate into behavior. Attitude plays a big role. Thus explanation of logical knowledge may not lead to as much behavioral change in students as attitude change will.

The formation of attitudes is much more intertwined with other factors such as beliefs, values, and moods. Let me illustrate my ideas with some examples.

Communication textbooks tell students that if they want to convey positive feedback in listening, they should sit up straight and lean forward a bit. What if the student does not believe in and have a negative attitude against the significance of an interest in others' minds? Does it really contribute to communication when one's leaning forward conveys a false image of positive listening which is *actually* hypocritical pseudo-listening? On the other hand, if a person *believes* in compassion, for example, which leads to a constant interest in his/her fellow human beings, does this person need the technical knowledge about how to convey a positive image in listening in order to engage in effective listening? What I mean is that effective communication comes more from a positive attitude than from knowledge of communicative concepts and skills. This is why I contend that the study of attitude is very important to the study of human communication.

I would like to give another example concerning effective public speaking or public persuasion in order to support my above contention. Many books have been published to teach people "skills" on how to give a persuasive public speech. The assumption is that these skills can build the reader into a more effective public speaker. The easiest way to refute this assumption is to study the biographies of the major effective public speakers in history. Such a study will reveal that what actually made these people successful public speakers was not a course in understanding communicative skills or a training in public speaking. What made them effective public speakers were their attitudes which, in turn, grew out of their strong beliefs. Even a strong belief in the irrational can produce a powerfully-driven attitude toward communication. Hitler was such an example. Any *skills* will prove effete when we face the problem of stage fright.

I want to diverge a little bit here in terms of coercion involved in school assignments, students' attitude toward school assignments, and the success of education as a cause of communication. If we consider the cause of education as an actual effort of communication, probably not enough attention is given to student attitudes toward this educational communication process. Many students, especially undergraduate students who constitute the bulk of college students, are not exhibiting a enthusiastic attitude toward school assignments. This attitude undoubtedly contributes to the widespread phenomenon of students' procrastination and boredom in dealing with school assignments. To increase the success of education as a cause of communication, a major task is to change student attitude toward school assignments. As demonstrated in the second paragraph of this paper, coercion decreases the possibility of attitude change. Does this reveal that student attitude is not changing enough toward more zeal to school assignments simply because too much coercion is involved in the design of school assignments? Probably. My contention is that more studies are merited to explore the connection between students' attitude toward school assignments and coercive factors involved in the design of school assignments, so that education as a cause of communication will become more successful.

In conclusion, if attitude affects behaviors, the study of human communication needs to shift its focus from skills to more psychological factors such as attitude.

Citations:

Braff, P. (1999, February 14). Washington in new portrayals. *New York Times* (Late Edition), P. 20.

Chambliss, Marilyn, J. & Garner, R. (1996). Do adults change their minds after reading persuasive text? *Written Communication, 13.* 291-313.

Roskos, E. & David, R. (1997). Implicit theories of persuasion. *Human Communicaiton Research, 24.* 31-63.

6

Scientism and Humanism—On Reading Weaver's Theory on Rhetoric

The rise of industrialization and technological application has led to scientism. This scientism, in turn, leads to the decline of rhetoric. The decline of rhetoric leads to widespread apathy in modern society. In order to achieve a better human condition, we need to re-emphasize the proper position of a proper rhetoric. This essay attempts to argue for the above contention through Weaver's theory on rhetoric.

Weaver argues nostalgically that the art of rhetoric, more than any other subject, has suffered a great decline. In the nineteenth century, the teacher of rhetoric had to be *somebody*, as Weaver said (Weaver, 1963, p. 1044). Now the teaching of rhetoric "is given to just about anybody who will take it" (Weaver, 1963, p. 1045). This decline of rhetoric, I believe, is caused by the rise of industrialization and then scientism. From mass production in industrialization, people saw the great producing power of efficiency which they could achieve from calculated mechanical organization of machines. Taylor was particularly inspired by the idea of efficiency. He believed that if compartmentalization and standardization could bring great efficiency out of machines, they should also be able to do so with humans. He immediately began seeing running cogs in human hands, transmission rods in human limbs, and control buttons in human eyes. Taylor believed that a meticulously calculated synchronization of these "cogs, rods, and buttons," scientifically embedded into automated mega-machines, would produce wonders. It all did. Work no longer was a cooperative effort, a way of life that gives a sense of community and sharing. Instead, work for many becomes a routine of very restricted content, an absolute evil to put up with for the acquisition of enough means to escape work. The concept of human is changed. The "changed concept of man [and woman] is best described by the word 'scientistic,' a term which denotes the application of scientific assumptions to subjects which are not wholly comprised of naturalistic phenomena" (Weaver, 1963, p. 1045). Social sciences, for instance, are already treating their subjects like this. Publications in social sciences focus their total attention on methodological provability than on humanistic significance. Your every argument has to be absolutely irrefutable. As a consequence, scholarship has become a dull accumulation of effete common sense packaged in arcane language for a scholarly flavor. Scholarship has become the epitome of logical and coherent nonsense, useful for nothing yet hard as rock to fight—how can you refute a person whose lips drip with words such as "perhaps," "maybe," "possibly," "presumably,".......

When efficiency becomes the over-ruling idea in our age, it "came to be believed increasingly that to think validly was to think scientifically, and that subject matters made no difference" (Weaver, 1963, 1045). What is produced no longer matters; only how much is produced (just look at the pattern of higher education). Logical validity has become the yardstick of scholarship. The scholar

> would work upon one thing as indifferently as upon another. He would be an eviscerated creature or a depassioned one, standing in the same relationship to the realities of the world as the thinking technique stands to the data on which it is employed. He would be a thinking robot, a concept which horrifies us precisely because the robot has nothing to think about (Weaver, 1963, p. 1047).

Many scholars can take any phenomenon in reality as the subject of her[1] study. After a logical processing of the collected data, she provides us with conclusions and discoveries. Moral philosophy and humanism are severed from many compartmentalized disciplines. These disciplines stand for their own sake, having nothing to do with the service of humankind. I consider Peter Ramus the forefather in establishing this modern thinking (1983). He uses even scientist method to deal with the humanist study of rhetoric and turns the full-fleshed rhetoric into a dry study of only delivery and style. In light with Ramus' philosophy, academic studies are becoming more compartmentalized purely for the sake of efficient scientistic development. Scholarly publications, educational classrooms, professorial lectures, none of them stirs the heart any longer. How can we expect them to change the world?

---

1. For mechanical convenience, this essay will use gender pronouns (he/she, his/her…) randomly.

Scientistic reasoning is replacing rhetorical reasoning in more and more areas of scholarship. Cause-effect analysis method is the major method for investigation scholars now use. According to Weaver, "cause and effect is a lower-order source of argument because it deals in the realm of the phenomenal" (Weaver, 1963, p. 1050). Since phenomena in this modern time have proliferated because of the emergence of numerous new technologies, scholarly study tends to make the world pile up "bodies of specialized knowledge which no one person can hope to command" (Weaver, 1963, p. 1050). To maintain objectivity in scholarship, many norms are stipulated, for instance, in terms of language. Weaver probably will not respond very positively to these norms, because he believes language itself is a "subjectively born, intimate, and value-laden vehicle" (Weaver, 1963, p. 1053). Also when the aim is to maintain scholastic objectivity through stipulations on language usage, we tend to ignore one fact that the scholar, when he does his research, is actually always selecting, emphasizing this and de-emphasizing that. We probably cannot achieve objectivity to a substantial degree without the scholar's personal honesty and her belief in the significance of her research conclusions. What helps is no longer norms (such as using "the author" instead of "I"). Our whole philosophy of what constitutes scholarship and how we evaluate professorial performance needs to be changed.

In contrast to scientism, rhetoric has become the "soft" study, which does not help quicker production at all. More students (and scholars), in choosing areas of study, tend to avoid anything rhetorical: human feelings, emotions, things difficult to logically define and mathematically quantify On the other hand, scientistic subjects, especially those which promise to generate more hard cash, have become more popular. Famous computer softwares will acquire much more attention than famous speeches, because the former addresses logically tangible and specific problems, and the latter is too much complicated, human, and holistic to be scholarly.

The consequence of the rise of scientism and the decline of rhetoric is widespread modern apathy. Humans, in nature, tend to be more rhetorical than logical. "Just what comprises humanism is not a simple matter for analysis. Rationality is an indispensable part to be sure, yet humanity includes emotionality, or the capacity to feel and suffer, to know pleasure, and it includes the capacity for aesthetic satisfaction, and what can be only suggested, a yearning to be in relation with something infinite" (Weaver, 1963, p. 1045). When people consider humanness as a drag on progress, human qualities as weaknesses, they have ignored the essence of humanity. Our scholarship mostly has become a dehumanized lifeless game of numbers, irrefutable nonsense, and a logical coherence of vacuities. Scholars may choose to ignore the humanness within themselves, but humanism does not simply go away because of your ignoring. Thus when people organize their lives mainly according to scientism, humanism is not lived in tranquility but pops up buoyantly. This conflict between scientism and humanism has led to ubiquitous boredom and ennui, in education, government, business, and even medicine. This world has become one of apathetic zombies. Students hate school. Employees hate work. Professors hate teaching. Work by no means is a pleasant concept, though inherently it is the only liberator of humanity. The University is longer the center of light, but the packaging house "of lost causes, and forsaken beliefs, and unpopular names, and impossible loyalties" (Mathew Arnold). Teachers ask their students to follow a valid reasoning without responding to reality. How can education hope to succeed by reasoning against reality?

Scientism tells us that calculated organization is good for production. Therefore, we try to organize everything neatly: college courses, schedules, work days and holidays, paper formats, entertainment, eating, sleeping…. Organization tries to make a "straight-cut ditch" of humanism which in its nature is "a free, meandering brook" (Thoreau). Educators tend to believe that the students will learn more and more if they are given and forced into more and more. Nothing can be further wrong. Students begin to *live* less and less with more and more to go through. Learning by no means is a matter of "going through or covering." Sensibility is surrendering to intelligence. "[T]things would be better if men [and women] did not give in so far to being human in the humanistic sense. In the shadow of the victories of science, his [or her] humanism fell into progressive disparagement" (Weaver, 1963, 1045). When humanism falls into progressive disparagement, our world becomes productive not of joy, but of pain, not of life, but of livelihood.

A re-emphasis on rhetoric may help lead us more toward humanism, and thus toward a better human condition for the individuals. Rhetoric "is addressed to man in his humanity" (Weaver, 1963, p. 1046). "[T]he most obvious truth about rhetoric is that its object is the whole man, his nature as a pathetic being, that is, a being feeling and suffering" (Weaver, 1963, p. 1046). "[O]rganizationl stewards need to be ever vigilant in supporting the humane use of human beings" (Van Patten, 1996, p. 79). Chancellor Emeritus William Pearson Tolley of Syracuse University wrote, "Education should deal with the whole [person]…. Schools and colleges should minister as best they can to the needs of the whole [person]" (cited in Van Patten, 1996, p. 84). Rhetoric has to re-assert its position for us to return to a proper concept of humanity, to realize that human is not so much a logical entity as an emotional one. We should reassure public speaking and famous speeches an important position in our education and life. The "rhetorical" studies address the person in its totality, thus in her humanness. Frequently I have to find inspiration for spiritual survival from famous speeches rather than from scholarly articles which just mercilessly destroy the human spirit. In my more than thirty years of learning and researching, I rarely come across a *scholarly* work that enlightens and stirs my heart. Much scholarship rather feels like works for mummies. Many great speeches, however, talk to me by addressing the reality of me as what I am. They talk about what I really feel. They talk about the mundane, the everyday life. They take into account my dreams, hopes, fears, and present circumstances. In one word, they talk to the real person. As Weaver says, "A speech intended to persuade achieves little unless it takes into account how men are reacting subjectively to their hopes and fears and their special circumstances" (Weaver, 1963, p. 1045).

Students and employees are not creatures "abstracted from time and place." Their lives are very much affected and molded by what happens in every minute and every location in their daily living. "If science deals with the abstract and the universal, rhetoric is near the other end, dealing in significant part with the particular and the concrete" (Weaver, 1963, p. 1046). Rhetoric "takes into account what science deliberately, to satisfy its own purposes, leaves out" (Weaver, 1963, p. 1046). That is, rhetoric takes humanism into its account. Rhetoric "always comes to us in well-fleshed words, and that is because it must deal with the world, the thickness, stubbornness, and power of it" (Weaver, 1963, p. 1047). Rhetoric embraces us not as resources for efficient production and targets for heedless consumption, but as the end for everything else and terminus of life. Rhetoric tries to restore dignity into the person by reminding him that he is a self-conscious individual with a lively human spirit. Rhetoric, with its holistic and stable voice, always tries to remind us where we truly want to go so that scientism, merely as the accelerator of the car of civilization, does not get us far off the proper track. One most important function of rhetoric in this age of reason is to protect reason from itself.

"Rhetoric seen in the whole conspectus of its function is an art of emphasis embodying an order of desire" (Weaver, 1963, p. 1048). Only when we address the desire can we get to address the soul; only when we address the soul can we get to address the person. Our education and professions need to address people's desire, to distinguish between the real desire from the soul and the false desire from the societal conditioning. We must use rhetoric as an antidote against the non-humanist scientism so that our organizational or societal life progresses in conformity with the individual in her real human desire.

"Either you change fast or you get crushed." This saying has become so popular nowadays. One of the greatest prophecies of our age is, "The greatest change of our age will be change itself." Let's see what Weaver has to say about change:

> The highest reality is being, not becoming.... That which is perfect does not change; that which has to change is less perfect. Therefore, if it is possible to determine unchanging essences or qualities and to speak in terms of these, one is appealing to what is most real in so doing. From another point of view, this is but getting people to see what is most permanent in existence, or what transcends the world of change and accident. The realm of essence is the realm above the flux of phenomena (Weaver, 1963, p. 1049).

Unfortunately, our scholarship is not clarifying the permanent essence of humanity, but fumbling with "the flux of phenomena." I consider the urge in social sciences to get to the new, the novel, the fleetingly unsaid, the smallest bit in the smallest abnormality as a bane rather than benefit. Rhetoric, in its highest form, tries to make people see the "unchanging essences" in human spirit. Once it succeeds in this, people will no longer struggle in order to keep their heads above the water of the flux of change; they will stay home with themselves. I hope the lost souls drifting on the sea will sooner find anchorage in their home.

Reference:

Ramus, P. (1983). Arguments in rhetoric against Quintillian (trans. Carole New-
lands, ed. James J. Murphy). In P. Bizzel & B. Herzberg (Eds.). (1990),
<u>The rhetorical tradition: Readings from classical times to the present</u> (pp.
1044-54). Boston: Bedford/St. Martin.

Van Patten, J. J. (1996). <u>The culture of higher education: A case study approach</u>.
Lanham, Maryland: University Press of America.

Weaver, R. (1963). Language is sermonic. In P. Bizzel & B. Herzberg (Eds.).
(1990), <u>The rhetorical tradition: Readings from classical times to the
present</u> (pp. 1044-54). Boston: Bedford/St. Martin.

7

Survey Report on the Topic of "Effective Leadership"

With our world becoming more and more complicated, scholars of organizational studies are realizing that management alone cannot solve our problems. More and more of their attention is turning to leadership, which, scholars believe, may promise a solution to the myriad of our problems. Many (e.g. Covey, 1996; Deming, 1993; and Senge, 1990) believe that management deals with the area of things, control, and efficiency, all of which only strike at the branches of the evil. Leadership, on the other hand, deals with the area of people, "release" (a tapping of the energy reservoir of the people, the opposite of the concept of "control", see for example Covey, 1996) and effectiveness, all of which represent an effort to strike at the root of the evil.

Although scholars have some agreement on leadership, there is not much congruence in their opinions on the question of what effective leadership is or what constitutes real leadership. After reading the prominent articles and books on this topic, I feel that four categories of ideas may emerge within the scholarly studies and opinions on leadership. Those that don't quite fit neatly into a specific category are usually a combination of two or more of these categories. These categories may be designated as the following: (1) Leaders are people who know what to do with themselves; (2) Leaders are people who know what to do with their people; (3) Leaders are people who know what to do with the communication channels/environment within their organizations; and (4) Leaders are people who have a holistic picture of what is going on there.

Before elaborating on each category of ideas, I'd like to talk a bit about how these four categories fit with each other. If you look at these categories from a bird's eye viewpoint, you will see that the first three make up the components of an organization—-the leader, the led, and the connection between them, i.e., the organizational communication channels. The fourth category is a synthesis of the first three, looking at the organization in a systemic manner.

1. Leaders are people who know what to do with themselves.

According to this category of thought, the leader leads by showing. In order to be able to lead by showing or modeling, the leader must have certain sets of personal characteristics. These characteristics make the leader the outstanding and visible person. One of the most important characteristics for effective leadership is personal mastery. That is, the leader has transcended the cacophony of reality and operates with the true and final/natural principles and laws, which represent the "truth" in people's hearts. Leaders are people "who have the vision, courage, and humility to constantly learn and grow" (Covey, 1996, p.149). Leaders are highly effective people powered by Covey's (1996) "Seven Habits": (1) Be proactive [personal vision]; (2) Begin with the end in mind [personal leadership]; (3) Put first things first [personal management]; (4) Think win-win [interpersonal leadership]; (5) Seek first to understand, then to be understood [empathic communication]; (6) synergize [creative cooperation]; and (7) Sharpen the saw [balanced self-renewal].

Heskett (1996) argues that leaders are "shapers" and "keepers" of their organizational culture. Ordinary people, judged against the standards of leadership by this school of thought, cannot be effective leaders, because leaders are an embodiment of high principles or natural laws (Covey, 1996). Because of being highly principle-centered, leaders act as compasses whereby the public navigate their lives. Thus, leaders are people with consistency between preach and practice, and with consistency in values and principles. Change and shift on the part of leaders can probably make the public feel "lost, confused, or fooled by conflicting voices and values" (Covey, 1996, p. 151). A "changeless, principle-centered core is the key to having the confidence, security, power, guidance, and wisdom," all of which are constitutive characteristics of leaders (Covey, 1996, p.151). Leadership, as showing, is a combination of character (who you are as a person) and competence (what you can do). The leader of the future has "a family within"—"humility and courage the parents, and integrity the child" (Covey, 1996, p.156). He has the humility to accept principles and the courage to align with them. This may take great personal sacrifice because of elements in reality that are not aligned with principles and natural laws. Out of this humility, courage, and sacrifice comes the person of integrity.

Leaders, according to Kanter (1996), have "an eye for change and a steadying hand to provide both vision and reassurance that change can be mastered, a voice that articulates the will of the group and shapes it to constructive ends, and an ability to inspire by force of personality while making others feel empowered to increase and use their own abilities" (p. 90). Kanter (1996) argues further that leaders should have not only the *vision*, but also the *ability* to show people that the vision can be made into reality. Thus leaders should have great brain-power "to imagine possibilities outside of conventional categories, to envision actions that cross traditional boundaries, to anticipate repercussion and take advantage of interdependencies, to make new connections or invent new combinations" (Kanter, 1996, p. 198).

Effective leaders should be able to define their employees' jobs in terms of identifying and constantly communicating commonly held values, shaping such values to enhance performance, ensuring the capability of people around them, living the commonly held values, listening a great deal of the time, and literally speaking a different language than their traditional counterparts. According to Farren and Kaye (1996), the leader is the facilitator, appraiser, forecaster, adviser, and enabler. According to Decrane, Jr. (1996), the leader, in character, should have knowledge of their duty, and a sense of honor in action; in vision, leaders should be able to spark the imagination of their people with a compelling vision of a worthwhile end that stretches the people beyond what is known today. Leaders also should be able to translate their vision into clear and realizable objectives. Leaders must have sufficient self-confidence to be willing to experience failure—in order ultimately to experience success. According to Bornstein and Anthony (1996), leaders are people with credibility. The credibility of leaders is based on Six C's:

1. Conviction: the passion and commitment the person demonstrates toward his or her vision.

2. Character: consistent demonstration of integrity, honesty, respect, and trust.

3. Care: demonstration of concern for the personal and professional well-being of others.

4. Courage: willingness to stand up for one's beliefs, challenge others, admit mistakes, and change one's own behavior when necessary.

5. Composure: consistent display of appropriate emotional reactions, particularly in tough or crisis situations.

6. Competence: proficiency in hard skills, such as technical, functional, and content expertise skills, and soft skills, such as interpersonal, communication, team, and organizational skills.

According to Melendez (1996), leaders are usually people of vision, effective communicators, effective decision-makers, and intelligent; they respect and value individuals and their dignity; they are committed to service and to obedience to the unenforceable; they have total honesty and integrity; they are kind; and they see themselves as teachers.

After reading this school of thought on leadership, you'll probably refrain from trying to be a leader, because leaders seem to be perfect people with all wonderful human characteristics. Yet I believe these reflections should also serve as directions of leadership endeavors.

2. Leaders are those who know how to expend their attention with the front-line people.

The leader is best when people barely know he exists.
   Not so good when people obey and acclaim him.
   Worse when they despise him.
   But of a good leader

   who talks little when his work is done,
   his aim fulfilled,
   they will say
   "We did it ourselves."

      Lao-tzu (604-531 B.C.)

According to this category of thought, the leader leads by understanding his/her people. The leader is not the hero or the outstanding person. He is the invisible person. The hero is the people. Heskett (1996) argued that effective leaders cannot attribute the organization's success to their brilliant leadership. It is the people of the organization and their feelings for customers and one another. All the leader has to do is to get the right people in the right job. According to this school of thought, the power of the leader does not come from his or her personal characteristics or charisma. The power comes from the leader's relations with the led or from the dignity the leader nurtures in those around him or her.

According to Helgesen (1996), good leadership lies in giving attention to the rank and file. They should realize that the success of the organization comes from the workers who possess specific sets of skills and varieties of expertise. Real leadership must take "power from the *head* of an organization and distribute it among those who comprise the *hands*...An organization cannot be truly responsive to the needs of those it is configured to serve unless its front-line people are given autonomy and support" (Helgesen, 1996, p. 21). If people feel as part of the corporate community, if they feel safe and cared for, if they are passionate about the mission and values and believe that others are living by them, they will generally give good service to the whole. The role of senior leadership will be like the role of the best kind of government of a free nation. By listening to their followers, these leaders will not be primarily players, or even coaches, but helpers to bring out the best in others. In an organization of effective leadership, everyone is the leader. In other words, leadership is seen in a culture or practices rather than in a single person or a small coterie of people.

Blanchard (1996) argues that the organizational pyramid should be turned upside down. The customers and the customer-contact people should be at the top of the pyramid. The top management is at the bottom. The top management works for the people in implementing visions and goals. That means the people are responsible and the top management is merely responsive. The task of the leader is simply to help the people to accomplish their goals. The leader is the cheerleader, supporter, and encourager rather than the judge, critic, or evaluator. Smith (1996) argues even a step further by saying that the leader should be the follower of his or her people by:

(1) Asking questions instead of giving answers.
(2) Providing opportunities for others to lead you (the leader).
(3) Doing real work in support of others instead of only the reverse.
(4) Becoming a matchmaker instead of a "central switch."
(5) Seeking common understanding instead of consensus.

In greatest contrast to traditional understanding of leadership are perhaps the ideas of O'Toole (1995), and Kouzes & Posner (1993). These scholars do not consider leaders as people in power and authority. Instead, leaders are servers for the people they lead. These researchers cite Jesus Christ as an example of a great leader. The power of Jesus comes not from giving orders to his people, but from understanding the needs and wishes of his people and from an effort to satisfy these needs and wishes.

3. Leaders are people who know what to do with the communication channels or environment within their organization.

According to this school of thought, effective leadership lies in the creation and maintenance of proper communication modes, patterns, and environment. What is fearful is not mistakes in the organizations or imperfections in the leaders or the people. What is fearful is clogged communication channels within the organization. Mumby (1984) argues that communication modes within an organization represent its power structure. Hierarchical construction of power surely prevents honest communication. He suggests open-ended interviews for enhancing honest communication within an organization. Although Mumby's article in 1993 is an effort to direct future critical organizational communication studies, its implication for leadership is clear. In order to tap the energy reservoir of the people, in order to lessen the tensions between individual values, choices, and goals on the one hand, and organizational values and goals on the other hand, leaders must give attention to the communication modes and channels in the organization, and design and create proper communication patterns. Schein (1993) argues that the root issue of leadership or effective organization lies at communication failures and misunderstandings. All these prevent parties from framing the problem in common ways, and thus make it impossible to deal with the problem constructively. At conferences, the leader should be the facilitator in maintaining effective dialogue instead of the order giver. Issacs (1993) believes that leaders should not hire their employees "from the neck down." They should allow the people to think by engaging them in productive dialogue, and by creating them a setting where people can surface fundamental assumptions and gain insight into why they arise.

McGill, Slocum, & Lei (1992) argue that leaders should maintain an open communication atmosphere within the organization by encouraging their people to express all perspectives on issues. Deming (1993) believed that the new leader at least has two roles in terms of communication. One, he or she should listen and learn without passing judgment on the people he or she listens. Two, the new leader will hold a conversation of four hours with every one of his or her people, at least once a year, not for judgment but merely to listen. Practically, this may be difficult to achieve in a large organization, but Deming's idea is clear. Senge (1990) contends that if "we'll just talk it out, we'll know what to do" (p. 218). "Visions that are genuinely shared require ongoing conversations where individuals not only feel free to express their dreams, but learn how to listen to each others' dreams. Out of this listening, new insights into what's possible gradually emerge" (Senge, 1990, p. 218). According to Harrison (1994), effective leadership should create a broad configuration of interaction in their organizations where things are less regulated by status considerations, and more by those related to knowledge and technical expertise. Within such organizations, there is a great emphasis on unhindered access to organizational information.

4. Effective leadership lies in maintaining a holistic or systemic picture of what is going on in their organizations.

This category of thought thinks that an effective leader is one who can make his/her organization function in a systemic manner. Every factor in the organization, including the leadership, the people, and other non-human parts, constitutes only as a component of the whole, which is the organization. According to Lippitt and Lippitt (1981), a system, in its simplest sense, is considered to be any entity composed of interdependent parts. The strength of the interdependence among a set of elements determines primary system characteristics such as centrality, cohesiveness, and coherence. Understanding the condition of a system is dependent on knowing the primary parts, the relationship that exists among them, and the forces that influence how they are modified.

Senge (1990) said that the unhealthiness of our world today is in direct proportion to our inability to see it as a whole. Deming (1993) called our present reality a prison created by the way in which people interact. If the system feels like a prison, wilting the plant of organizational life instead of watering it, no individual within the organization can be liberated or enlivened. The system is like the sun. The individual people within this organization are like plants that cannot escape the omnipresence of the sun.

Role number two of the new manager or leader, according to Deming (1993), is to help his/her people see themselves as a component in a system. Senge (1990) contends that we usually focus on obvious symptoms, not on underlying causes. Systemic thinking means a shift of mind from seeing parts to seeing the whole, from seeing people as helpless reactors to seeing them as active participants in shaping their reality, from reacting to the present to creating the future. True understanding comes from studying how we together contribute to our own problems in a systematic manner. This is also what Deming (1993) called the "stable system of defects," meaning that defects in products and service do not come from people, but only derive from the holistic functioning of the system. Senge's (1990) frog parable[1] shows that we create our problems so gradually that when we actually come to the stage of having the problems, we no longer can recall how we created them in the first place. "Once structures are recognized, it becomes possible to begin to alter structures to free people from previously mysterious forces that dictated their behavior" (Senge, 1990, p.190). Senge continues to argue that the reason why structural/systemic explanations are so important is that only they address the underlying causes of behavior at a level that *patterns* of behavior can be changed. Systems thinking simplifies life by helping us see the deeper patterns lying behind the events and the details. What we usually do in reality, on the other hand, is analyze and divide the problem into small parts and try to solve the problem by striving for solutions to each part; what we usually do is pushing harder and harder on familiar solutions, while fundamental problems persist or worsen. And this is a reliable indicator of non-systemic thinking—the so-called 'what-we-need-here-is-a-bigger-hammer' syndrome. This school of thought on leadership contends that systems thinking is very important in solving problems, and that effective leadership lies in maintaining systems thinking and practice.

After reading all the ideas on leadership, I personally tend to conclude that a real leader is one who is great in vision but humble in spirit. On the one hand, the leader should understand very well how our own actions and attitudes contribute systematically to our own problems and how various forces can be aligned to fulfill instead of defeat *our* (instead of *my*) aspirations. On the other hand, the leader should be able to transcend socially constructed fashions and pose himself as a model for better human development by serving and sacrificing for his/her fellow people.

---

1. According to Senge's frog parable, if you put a frog in a container and increase the temperature in the container very gradually, the frog will not feel the small temperature increases and thus will not do any adaptive actions, until it finally dies of high temperature.

References:

Blanchard, K. (1996). Turning the organizational pyramid upside-down. In Hesselbein, F., Goldsmith, M., & Beckhard, R. (Eds.), The leader of the future (pp. 81-86). San Francisco: Jossey-Bass.

Bornstein, S. M. & Smith, A. F. (1996), The puzzles of leadership. In Hesselbein, F., Goldsmith, M., & Beckhard, R. (Eds.), The leader of the future (pp. 281-292). San Francisco: Jossey-Bass.

Covey, S. R. (1996). Three roles of the leader in the new paradigm. In Hesselbein, F., Goldsmith, M., & Beckhard, R. (Eds.), The leader of the future (149-159). San Francisco: Jossey-Bass.

Deming, W.E. (1993). The new economics. Cambridge, MA: Massachusetts Institute of Technology, Center for Advanced Engineering Study.

Decrane, A. C. Jr. (1996), A constitutional model of leadership. In Hesselbein, F., Goldsmith, M., & Beckhard, R. (Eds.), The leader of the future (pp. 249-256). San Francisco: Jossey-Bass.

Farren, C. & Kaye, B. L. (1996). New skills for new leadership roles. The leader of the future (pp. 175-188). In Hesselbein, F., Goldsmith, M., & Beckhard, R. (Eds.) San Francisco: Jossey-Bass.

Harrison, T. M. (1994). Communication and interdependence in "democratic organizations." In S. Deetz (Ed.), Communication Yearbook 17 (pp. 247-274). Thousand Oaks, CA: Sage.

Helgesen, S. (1996), Leading from the grassroots. In Hesselbein, F., Goldsmith, M., & Beckhard, R. (Eds.), The leader of the future (pp. 19-24). San Francisco: Jossey-Bass.

Heskett, J. L. & Schlesinger, L. A. (1996). Leaders who shape and keep performance-oriented culture. In Hesselbein, F., Goldsmith, M., & Beckhard, R. (Eds.), The leader of the future (pp. 111-120). San Francisco: Jossey-Bass.

Isaacs, W. N. (1993). Taking flight: Dialogue, collective thinking and organizational learning. Organizational Dynamics, 22, 24-39.

Kanter, R. M. (1996). World-class leaders: The power of partnering. In Hessel-bein, F., Goldsmith, M., & Beckhard, R. (Eds.), The leader of the future (pp. 89-98). San Francisco: Jossey-Bass.

Kouzes, J. M. & Posner, B. Z. (1993). Credibility: How leaders gain and lose it, why people demand it. San Francisco: Jossey-Bass.

Lippitt, R. & Lippitt, G. (Eds.). (1981). Systems thinking—A resource for orga-nization diagnosis and intervention. Washington, D.C.: International Consultants Foundation.

McGill, M.E., Slocum, J.W., & Lei, D. (1992). Management practices in learn-ing organizations. Organizational Dynamics, 22, 5-17.

Melendez, S. E. (1996). An "outsider's" view of leadership. In Hesselbein, F., Goldsmith, M., & Beckhard, R. (Eds.), The leader of the future (pp. 293-302). San Francisco: Jossey-Bass.

Mumby, D.K. (1984). Ideology and power in organization. Unpublished doc-toral dissertation, Southern Illinois University.

Mumby, D. K. (1993). Critical organizational communication studies: The next 10 years. Communication Monographs, 60, 18-25.

O'Toole, J. (1995). Leading change: Overcoming the Ideology of Comfort and the tyranny of custom. San Francisco: Jossey-Bass.

Schein, E. H. (1993). On dialogue, culture and organizational learning. Organi-zational Dynamics, 22, 40-51.

Senge, P. M. (1990). The fifth discipline. New York: Doubleday.

8

Personal Transformation and Organizational Effectiveness

People can face almost any problem except the problems of people. If we don't change (or "restore") people, we change little. If we have the courage of choosing to see the truth of current condition in education, business, and government, we have the power to change ourselves profoundly.

The term "personal transformation" may sound abstract. Let me put it this way. Personal transformation is something needed when life is felt not one of joy but one of task. It is something we need when we feel "we work in order to earn the income to do what we really want when we are not working." Personal transformation is an idea of quality instead of one of quantity; an idea of the standard of life instead of the standard of living; an idea of action instead of one of reaction (by action, I mean that which is done with a voluntary will; by reaction, I mean that which is stimulated by an external stimulus). What personal transformation tries to give is a journey of joyful harmony instead of one of competitive strife (Someone said, "The problem with the rat race is that even if we win in the race, we are still rats." That is, we remain untransformed.). Personal transformation is an idea of cooperation instead of one of competition. To make the long-winded arguments short, personal transformation is a need acutely felt and a wish urgently aspired. The purpose of personal transformation is to tap the reservoirs latent in ourselves that we have thoughtlessly severed from us. To people with a high level of personal transformation, a vision is a calling rather than simply a good idea. They are connected to others and to life itself (Yet reality is different—everyone is doing his own business without knowing interactions of the large components in their organization; work and life are scarcely united into one). They feel as if they are part of a larger creative process, which they can influence but cannot unilaterally control. When we are personally transformed, we give attention not so much to efficiency, success, and winning as to how we really feel about and experience life because "full emotional development offers the greatest degree of leverage in attaining our full potential."

If we are personally transformed, practicing the virtues of life and business success are not only compatible but enrich one another. The is a far cry from the traditional morals of the marketplace (The business man should be crafty. If you don't destroy your competitor, you'll get destroyed.). Max de Pree, retired CEO of Herman Miller, speaks of a "covenant" between the organization and the individual, in contrast to the traditional "contract" ("an honest day's pay in exchange for an honest day's work"). "Contracts," says De Pree, "are a small part of a relationship. A complete relationship needs a covenant...a covenantal relationship rests on a shared commitment to ideas, to issues, to values, to goals, and to management processes...Covenantal relationships reflect unity and grace and poise. They are expressions of the sacred nature of relationships."

Steps of Personal Transformation:

The result of personal transformation is the establishment of a systemic view, which depends on a shared vision, which in turn depends on the clarification of personal vision or values. Why so? Because when we are clear about the personal vision or values or what is really important to the individual, we realize that we are inherently the same as a group, and thus a shared vision appears, and thus a systemic view appears. And when a systemic view appears, our personal vision or values get fulfilled the best. So personal transformation starts with the clarification of personal visions or values and ends with the fulfillment of these visions and values. For the clarification of personal vision or values and the establishment of the shared vision, we need three steps: (1) learning how to reflect on tacit assumptions; and (2) expressing one's vision and listening to others' visions, and (3) joint inquiry into different people's views of current reality.

Personal Visions or Values:

We have goals and objectives, but these are not visions. Senge in his popular work, the Fifth Discipline said, "When personal transformation becomes a discipline—an activity we integrate into our lives—it embodies two underlying movements. The first is continually clarifying what is important to us. Personal transformation means not acquiring more information, but expanding the ability to produce the results we truly want in life. We often spend too much time coping with problems along our path that we forget why we are on that path in the first place. The result is that we only have a dim, or even inaccurate, view of what's really important to us. The second is continually learning how to see current reality more clearly. We've all known people entangled in counterproductive relationships, who remain stuck because they keep pretending everything is all right. Or we have been in business meetings where everyone says, 'We're on course relative to our plan,' yet an honest look at current reality would show otherwise. In moving toward a desired destination, it is vital to know where you are now" (p. 147).

"The discipline of personal mastery/transformation starts with clarifying the things that really matter to us, of living our lives in the service of our highest aspirations" (Senge, p. 7). Generative learning occurs only when people are striving to accomplish something that matters deeply to themselves, something that betters human condition over time. A vision not consistent with values that people live by day by day will not only fail to inspire genuine enthusiasm, it will often foster outright cynicism. Vision, values and purpose are interdependent. "The ferment in management will continue until we build organizations that are more consistent with man's [and woman's] higher aspirations beyond food, shelter and belonging" (Senge, p.148). The ability to focus on ultimate intrinsic desires, not only on secondary goals, is a cornerstone of personal transformation. Real vision cannot be understood in isolation from the idea of purpose. By purpose, I mean an individual sense of why she is alive. Happiness may be most directly a result of living consistently with your purpose. George Bernard Shaw expressed the idea pointedly when he said, "This is the true joy in life, the being used for a purpose recognized by yourself as a mighty one…'" "The same principle has been expressed in some organizations as 'genuine caring'…When people genuinely care, they are naturally committed. They are doing what they truly want to do. They are full of energy and enthusiasm. They persevere, even in the face of frustration and setbacks, because what they are doing is *their work*."

If we don't clarify what we truly seek, we may reach all our goals and objectives without feeling any sense of fulfillment, satisfaction, and joy. When we are unclear between interim goals and more intrinsic goals, the subconscious has no way of prioritizing and focusing. Purpose and vision are intrinsic not relative. It's something you desire for its own sake, not because where it stands you relative to other people. The intrinsic produces voluntary action that says, "I want to do it. You want to do it. S/he wants to do it. Let's do it together for ourselves." The relative produces competition that says, "I will do better than you and win for myself." So vision and purpose produce cooperation and harmony, and lack of purpose and vision or competition produces struggle, frustration, and disorientation. Purpose and vision make us wish for longer days; competition make us wish for holidays. Senge said, "For the American, time is the enemy. For the Japanese, time is an ally." In order to avoid competition and frustration, W. Edwards Deming opposed setting quotas and goals for workers and opposed our current grading system to students. Competition makes people live in fear of failure. And Deming wrote pages and pages to show how bad and constraining fear is. In one word, clarification of personal vision and values unites and offers joy. Ambiguity about them divides and causes pain.

My reading of Deming and Senge tends to give me the conclusion that the real value directs us to a life of joy and fulfillment, not a life of task and pressure. We must work at learning how to separate what we truly want, from what we think needs to be done in order to achieve it. One of the greatest tragedies for us is that many historical practices, once used only as means for the stable purpose, eventually become purposes themselves that lead us further astray from what we really want. Frustration and fatigue then inevitably emerge.

What do we want? It is a serious question needing serious study. Some obvious examples are: We want joy instead of pain; we want atomic energy instead of A-bomb; from education; we want enjoyment of personal growth, not continual completion of homework, if the homework does not contribute to the personal growth. But reality doesn't seem to be what we wish for. Deming gives us the idea of rugged individualism, which means self-determination, joy in learning, joy in work, a feeling in anyone that he is responsible to himself, with only himself to satisfy. And he went on, "The present style of reward has crushed the [rugged] individual." The crushed individual is rather like a "zombie," active with his/her hands but with numbed mind and a callused heart. Zombies in the workplace are employed only with their hands and heels but never with their hearts and minds. Imagine the waste if you pay your employees only for their hands and heels. Our current work system is in a crisis (refer to Deming's *Out of the Crisis*). Something needs to be changed. And Deming and Senge said: No, it's not a matter of change. It is a matter of transformation. In Deming's eye, we need a new system of profound knowledge to replace our current system of spurious evaluations.

Developing a More Systemic Worldview:

The unhealthiness of our world today is in direct proportion to our inability to see it as a whole. Deming called our present system a prison created by the way in which people interact and evaluate each other (*The New Economics*. p. xi). If the system feels like a prison that wilts the plant of life instead of watering it, no individual plant of life can be liberated or enlivened. Without personal transformation on the part of both the leader and the masses, we won't be able to change the system. Personal transformation and systemic thinking are one idea.

Role #2 of the new manager, according to Deming, is to help the group see themselves as a component in a system. Senge contends that we usually focus on obvious symptoms, not on underlying causes. Systemic thinking means a shift of mind from seeing parts to seeing the whole, from seeing people as helpless reactors to seeing them as active participants in shaping their reality, from reacting to the present to creating the future. True understanding comes from how we contribute to our own problems. If we really have met the enemy, we'll realize it is us. Senge's frog parable shows us that we create our problems so gradually that when we actually come to the stage of the problems, we no longer can recall how we ourselves created them in the first place (refer to p. 160 of *Fifth Discipline*). "Once structures are recognized, it becomes possible to begin to alter structures to free people from previously mysterious forces that dictated their behavior." "The reason that structural/systemic explanations are so important is that only they address the underlying causes of behavior at a level that *patterns* of behavior can be changed. Systems thinking simplifies life by helping us see the deeper patterns lying behind the events and the details. Yet what we usually do is analyze and divide the problem into small parts and try to offer solutions to each part; what we usually do is "pushing harder and harder on familiar solutions, while fundamental problems persist or worsen. And this is a reliable indicator of nonsystemic thinking—what we often call 'what we need here is a bigger hammer' syndrome." This is what happens in millions of Chinese organizations, business, governmental or educational. In China, all levels of state-owned organizations have the weekly political study, in which we read and listen to articles and speeches from the central government. I personally have been doing this since when I was an elementary schoolboy. Yet the years of the political study left in my mind nothing but boredom and apathy. And everybody felt so. The ideas and even the wording of the articles and speeches almost never change. People see no connection between their reality and the political study. Yet the government never stopped building the hammer of political study to make it bigger and bigger. And it never worked. Imposing ideas from top never change, much less transform, people. They only deform people, making them more alienated and apathetic. Our solutions may lead to solving a problem, but it will not change the thinking that produced the problem.

Building a Shared Vision from Personal Vision:

Role #1 of a manager of people, according to Deming, is: A manager and his people understand the meaning of a system. They understand how the work of the group may support the aims of the system. The loyalty of Spartacus' army was not to Spartacus, the man. Their loyalty was to a shared vision which Spartacus had inspired—the idea that they could be free men. Shared vision is the most powerful human force. They create a sense of commonality that permeates the organization and gives coherence to diverse activities. Maslow observed that in exceptional teams, "the task was no longer separate from the self...but rather he identified with this task so strongly that you couldn't define his real self without including that task" (Senge, *Fifth Discipline*, p.206). Today, "vision" is a familiar concept in corporate leadership. But when you look carefully, you find that most "visions" are one person's (or one group's) goals imposed on an organization. Such visions, at best, command compliance—not commitment. A shared vision is a vision that many people are truly committed to, because it reflects their own personal vision. Organizational vision or shared vision are not in conflict with personal vision which is the bedrock for developing a shared vision.

Human nature is to work and create, instead of avoiding work—This should be the basis for developing any shared organizational vision. "Throughout history, almost every culture has had art, music, dance, architecture, poetry, storytelling, pottery, and sculpture. The desire to create is not limited by beliefs, nationality, creed, educational background, or era. The urge resides in all of us...it is not limited to the arts, but can encompass all of life, from the mundane to the profound." Deming, when interviewed, said, "Human nature is not laziness. We are born with a wish to work and to create." There is a burning need for people to feel part of an ennobling mission. If it is absent, many will seek fulfillment only in interests outside instead of within their work.

When it comes to *system*, most people feel frustrated, powerless, and hopeless, because the system is considered a thing of monstrous size that is external, uncontrollable, and hostile. Yet Senge said, "We are part of the structure. This means that we often have the power to alter structures within which we are operating. However, more often than not, we do not perceive that power. In fact, we usually don't see the structure [or system] at play much at all. Rather, we just find ourselves feeling compelled to act in certain ways." "Reality is created by ourselves. It is not simply a reified, unchanging structure...[Yet] This reality is often taken for granted, or made to be taken for granted by power groups through metaphors, propaganda, etc." For personal transformation, we a combination of the *Mao* and the *Deng*. Mao Zedong was an idealist ("We want everything socialist, even if it is a weed; we refuse anything capitalist, even if it is a good seedling.). Deng Xiaoping was a pragmatist (A cat, white or black, is a good one as long as it catches the rats). Both revolution (Maoism) and evolution (Dengism) should be at work. Maslow found that one of the most distinguishing characteristics of healthy people was their ability to live comfortably with seeming opposites. Such comfort is indeed one of the outcomes of personal transformation. We have many cynics in our lives. Cynics are not people personally transformed. Scratch the surface of most cynics and you find a frustrated idealist—someone who made the mistake of converting his ideals into expectations without adequate attention to incremental implementation of plans. Hanover's Bill O'Brien points out that "burnout" comes from causes other than simply working too hard. "There are teachers, social workers, and clergy," says O'Brien, "who work incredibly hard until they are 80 years old and never suffer "burnout"—because they have an accurate view of human nature. They don't over-romanticize people, and they are people with idealistic visions *and* realistic methods.

Personal Transformation on the Part of the Leaders:

Managers' fundamental task is "providing the enabling conditions for people to lead the most enriching lives they can." Deming also admonished: Don't rush people. Don't give quotas. Offer people the best conditions including the equipment, materials, and instruments and make them find pride in their workmanship. Be a model: Commit yourself to your own personal transformation. Talking about personal transformation may open people's minds somewhat, but actions always speak louder than words. There's nothing more powerful you can do to encourage others in their quest for personal transformation than be serious in your own quest. So long as the leader continues to be the model, her work habits will set the norm. Give attention to power structures also because the masses' participation is only realized through actual change in the structure of power relations.

Two tools for the clarification of personal vision or values and the establishment of the shared vision:

(1) **Learning how to reflect on tacit assumptions or mental models.** Behind our words and actions, there are always assumptions. The problem-solving pro-

cess won't be improved until we get in touch with our own and each others' assumptions. Our beliefs are heavily contaminated with unconscious and invisible "programs" that came from others, history, or the system. We *can* move beyond those limiting assumption, but we must be willing to challenge ourselves and do the inner work of finding our real wishes that lie buried beneath the cultural overlay and cacophony of the daily practices. The problem with mental models is that we remain unaware of our mental models, which then remain unexamined, which then remain unchanged. Yet they are a great invisible hand. What we need here is deconstruction of the reality. Personal transformation requires the evolution of shared mental models. Senge suggests four points to dig out our mental models: (a) Recognizing "leaps of abstraction" (noticing our jumps from observation to generalization); (b) Exposing the "left-hand column" (articulating what we normally do not say in our mouth and even in our heart); (c) Balancing inquiry and advocacy: advocacy tries to convince and tends to make communication lapse into a debate, and inquiry builds a common experience base that allows us to learn collectively. Suspend judgment and listen because suspension of judgment allows for reflection); (d) Facing up to the gap between espoused theories (what we say) and theories-in-use (the implied theory in what we do). Mental models should lead to self-concluding decisions to work their best. As long as openness of communication is encouraged and practiced, people will find it a bit easier to cope with the gap between espoused theory and practiced theory in their daily reality.

(2) Expressing one's vision and listening to others' visions, and joint inquiry into different people's views of current reality. (a) Openness: Learning requires that managers be truly open to the widest possible range of perspectives in order to identify trends and generate choices. Openness serves as an antidote against "the disease of game-playing" that dominates people's behavior in face-to-face meetings. Nobody described an issue at 10:00 AM at a business meeting the way they described the issue at 7:00 in the evening, at home or over drinks with friends. Here everyone makes his or her thinking explicit and subject to public examination. To achieve openness, no judgment is to be meted out. Role #5 of the new manager, according to Deming, is coach and counsel, not a judge. Real change does not happen until people feel psychologically safe. In real communication, all participants must regard one another as colleagues. This is perhaps why Deming is against ranking and grading. Yet the reality is that "it becomes a cultural rule to say something nice if you say anything at all, and if you can't say something nice, don't say anything." When judgment is involved in communication, we reduce opportunities for learning about the reality that is actually there. **(b) Merit:** Making decisions based on the best interests of the organization was Hanover's antidote to "decision-making based on bureaucratic politics, where the name of the game is getting ahead by making an impression, or, if you're already at the top, staying there. **(c) "Dialogue":** Dialogue gives the capacity to members of a team to suspend assumptions and enter into a genuine "thinking together" (Thinking is different from thought: thoughts are what we have now as opinions, yet thinking is to examine how our perceptions and cognitions are preformed by our past experience). An important goal of dialogue is to enable the group to reach a higher level of consciousness and creativity through the gradual creation of a shared set of meanings and a 'common' thinking process.

Roles 13 and 14 of the new manager (by Deming) are: (13) [The manager] listens and learns without passing judgment on him that he listens. (14) He will hold a conversation of four hours with every one of his people, at least once a year, not for judgment but merely to listen. Why four hours, because dialogue emphasizes the natural flow of conversation; if a strict agenda is given, people in the dialogue will compete for a share of the airtime. Mumby suggests open-ended interviews for clarifying personal visions. "All problem-solving groups should begin in a dialogue format to facilitate the building of sufficient common ground and mutual trust, and to make it possible to tell what is really on one's mind." According to Heisenberg, science is rooted in conversations. The cooperation of different people may culminate in scientific results of the utmost importance. Dialogue is a visioning process which inquires into the future we truly seek to create. The belief that "we'll just talk it out and we'll know what to do" turns out to be a cornerstone of "dialogue." Visions that are genuinely shared require ongoing conversations where individuals not only feel free to express their dreams, but learn how to listen to each other's dreams. Out of this listening, new insights into what's possible gradually emerge.

The Results of Personal Transformation:

In a transformed society, the individuals work toward a greater society instead of a more successful self measured through insensible and uneconomic evaluation systems. People don't get judged and stratified. Rather, people are valued instead of evaluated, valued for the pursuit of their personal joy which is largely in accordance with the welfare of the greater society. Practices are integrated with reason. Continual connectedness with rather than a hopeless isolation from the world is felt. Minimized is the gap between individual aspirations and organizational goals. People with high levels of personal transformation cannot afford to choose between reason and intuition, or head and heart, any more than a normal person could choose to walk on one leg or see with one eye. A transformed society is one of joy and peace, the ultimate success of all successes.

References:

Deming, W.E. (1986). Out of the crisis. Cambridge, MA: Center for Advanced Engineering Study (MIT).

Deming, (1993). The new economics. Cambridge, MA: Center for Advanced Engineering Study (MIT).

Espejo, R. (1994). What is systemic thinking? System Dynamics Review, 10, 199-212.

Hesselbein, F., Goldsmith, M. & Beckhard, R. (Eds.) (1996). The leader of the future. San Francisco: Jossey-Bass.

Isaacs, W.N. (1993). Taking flight: Dialogue, collective thinking and organizational learning. Organizational Dynamics, 22, 24-39.

Kilman, R. H., Kilman, I., & associates. (1994). Managing ego energy: The transformation of personal meaning into organizational success. San Francisco: Jossey-Bass.

Mumby, D.K. (1984). Ideology and power in organization. Unpublished doctoral dissertation, Southern Illinois University-Carbondale.

Schein, E.H. (1993). On dialogue, culture and organizational learning. Organizational Dynamics, 22, 40-51.

Senge, P. M. (1990). The fifth discipline. New York: Doubleday.

9

How Communication Empowers Change

In my conviction, a desire for change for the better is embedded in human nature. We always tend to seek novelty: We invent new words and art forms; we leave our birthplaces to seek better lives elsewhere; we easily get bored with the same taste of the same food; we harbor a constant, undeniable desire for the new and the different.

But why change, especially social changes, have become so difficult that they border on the impossible? Why people resist change at seemingly whatever cost—draconian, stifling regulations, boring routines and formalities, and blood-shedding wars? Why? A desire to answer this question prompted James O'Toole to have written the wonderful book, *Leading Change.*

Despite my great admiration to O'Toole, I disagree with him upon a basic point. He seems to believe that the greatest resistance to change is the despot of custom, and that it is almost an ingrained element in human nature to maintain the custom. I am convinced, on the other hand, that the greatest resistance to change is the despot of irrational social power and entrenched practices, and that it is an ingrained element in human nature to seek change. Since any argument concerning human nature is usually very unfruitful, I will concentrate my arguments on how irrational social power resists change, and how communication will empower me to overcome this irrational power in order to be able to lead change.

The irrational social power has injected a basically wrong conception into people that joy of one group has to be based on the pain of another, and that success of one thing has to be based on the failure of another. The joy of the CEO has to be based on the pain of his/her people accepting the draconian discipline and working diligently against their private rationality and passion. The success of the professional has to be based on the failure of the father/the wife. The mentality of win-lose mentality is not only endorsed but practiced everywhere in education, business, and government. In line with this wrong mentality, changes to one thing never fail to cause failure to another, changes to one group never fail to cause pain to another group. This is why changes never fail to become repugnant to some people who naturally will resist these changes.

Communication is the only tool and yet a powerful tool to liberate the private rationality that advocates joy based on pain to none and success based no failure to none. Joy based on no pain and success based on no failure is distilled into values. Values are inclusionary in that they treat everyone equally. To values, there are no exceptions. Thus values simplify and yet are so dynamic as to be adaptable to all circumstances. Contingency rules, on the other hand, represents joy for one group based on pain to another group and success for one group based on failure to another group. Contingency rules are exlusionary in that people and situations should be categorized and treated differently and unequally. To contingency rules, exceptions are everywhere. Thus contingency rules complicate and yet static—a new key has to be found for every new lock.

To effect real changes, value-based changes, changes that people do not resist, the leader has to actually experience people's pain, clarify people's pain, and then show how to overcome their pain. Without experiencing the people's pain, the leader will not be able to connect with the people; without being able to clarify the pain, the leader will not win confidence of the people; without being able to show how to overcome the pain, the leader will not gain the following of the people. If the leader can communicate to the people that he has experienced the pain, has understood the pain, and has found the way to overcome the pain, the leader will gain natural followership who embrace changes instead of resist changes.

Citations:

O'Toole, J. (1996). <u>Leading change: The argument for values-based leadership</u>. San Francisco: Jossey-Bass.

10

Humor in the Multicultural Experience

Humor is deployed for achieving quite specific purposes such as face-saving, self-preservation, tension-relieving, and getting things done. Humor can be used as a sword: to influence and persuade, to motivate and unite, to speak the unspeakable and to facilitate desired change. Humor can also be used as a shield: to deflect criticism, to cope with failure, to defuse tension and to beguile the boring life. The use of humor is to break down barriers and to establish intimacy (either ephemeral or everlasting), which may precipitate the fructification of efforts. Humor is not merely a gimmick to beget laughter. Humor is the good nature saying, "I want to know you, to be closer to you, to feel an affinity between us."

A person in a new culture may feel isolated and sequestered, severed from his or her familiarities. Life in the new culture may feel like one of void and vacuum. Familiar references from the old culture are no longer dependable as guidance. This, ironically, may produce a freed feeling as well as a bewildered one. Why a freed feeling? One, others may judge you kindly or give you the benefit of doubt, knowing that you are from a different culture. Two, you may lavishly fall back on the universal principle for multicultural experience—the instinct of good nature or humor. Dependence on good nature alone may make you say and do funny or puzzling things in a foreign land. Your mouth may spout offensive words, and yet your face radiates with polite and good-natured smiles. Relevant to this, I experienced an interesting incident. One day, I saw a Chinese student buying food at McDonald's in the Student Center. He said to the waitress, "You, sucker." The waitress quickly appeared puzzled and offended. My instinct in the language of Chinese immediately enabled me to realize what the Chinese student wanted. He wanted a straw—something with which he could *suck* the beverage. This Chinese student may have felt lucky having me nearby who helped explain what he really wanted. The waitress quickly changed her attitude after the clarification. She was not too "serious" about the incident. To facilitate intercultural communication, a "humoristic" attitude from both the host and the guest is helpful. A "humoristic" attitude is characterized by curiosity for the amusing side of messages. A simplistic attitude, however, does not help. This attitude is characterized, however, by a mechanical response to any external stimulus.

When visiting or receiving a new culture, that is, when experiencing some "cultural vacuum," we must learn to molt our indigenous values and assumptions, and resort to the more universal value of good nature or humor. We must learn to be less critical of, more sensitive to, and more receptive of diversity. For one reason, you may simply not have enough time to criticize diversity that is omnipresent around you. Diversity and harmony should not be pitted against each other. We may reap a stronger sense of harmony and bond of humanity when we value diversity and respect others' differences. Again, adopt the "humoristic" attitude. A humoristic attitude may enable us to feel the "romance" in a multicultural context. It is romantic to interact with people of differences. Learning happens much more easily in this interaction than in one with people you are too familiar with. This may be the reason why some marriages end in divorce—boredom and ennui.

11

Barriers to Genuine Communication

1. when conformity to power is expected;

2. when negative judgment is possible;

3. when preconceptions are involved;

4. when communication becomes a task because of obligation to conform to certain communication rituals/manners;

5. when communication is not likely to produce any results;

6. when the environment is value-laden (this is why strangers may find it easier to self-disclose to each other);

7. when taboos are likely to be involved;

8. when the mind is preoccupied with a certain agenda or immediate personal problems and the communication is not relevant to the agenda and problems;

PART II

Education and Scholarship

1

The Purpose of Social Sciences and the Current Condition of Scholarship

Social sciences, different from natural sciences, are not a matter of discovery and invention, but a matter of clarification and implementation. The subject of natural sciences is the external—the nature and environment. The subject of social sciences, on the other hand, is the internal—us. For social sciences, we must listen carefully to what we consciously think and aspire. Much of this is achievable in a conscious solitude. For discovery of many of the truths about human nature, intuition and logic may be adequate. This is why fundamental human truths were discovered and so eloquently reified long ago by ancient Greeks.

Somehow, modern scholars of social sciences have long developed a distrust of human intuition, feeling, emotion, and simple logic. Every truth, however obvious and self-evident, must be proved. And statistical proof has almost become the sole accepted proof. I have been reviewer for numerous scholarly associations and publications. Much of the scholarship in those submitted papers appalled as to the current condition of our scholarship. As I remember, one paper spent twenty pages of immaculate reasoning and statistical report and analysis to discover the exciting conclusion that "students with 24-hour Internet access tend to use the Internet more often than those who don't have 24-hour access." Not only unpublished papers, but publications from respected journals cannot but appall me as to what we are doing with our best minds of the professors, the prime years of these talents, and public money by students and tax-payers. In one of the most prestigious journals in the field of communication (For self-protection, forgive me for not giving the name of the journal, although I can cite the exact page numbers), I found the following arguments, "Dyadic relationships are embedded within a larger social context and that this embeddedness creates the possibility that dyadic relationships influence and are influenced by that larger context." I'm wondering what can be inane than this kind of argument. Strip it of some the fancy words, it is no more fancier than saying, "People who are more friendly to each other *tend* to smile to each other more." Scholars are never wrong. How can they; they never make any argument with any certitude. Words of probability (such as perhaps, maybe, possibly, presumably,...) are the shield of scholarship. Our scholarship is immaculately correct and logical and but so much vacuous. Throughout my more than thirty years of academic life as a student and a professor, I can't hardly remember any scholarly journal article in social science that ever stirred any string of my heart. Much scholarship, in my experience, is nothing but a marathon of mental numbness and coherent nonsense packaged in the recycled paper of esoteric language.

Students are tortured everywhere by elaborated nonsense in commercial textbooks, hardly any of which edify and educate. How can they; first of all, they can hardly keep the students awake.

Our scholars are no longer great teachers. The bulk of them have become hairsplitting petty-foggers. Our scholarship no longer enlightens, enriches, and unites. It rather departmentalizes and debilitates. Communication scholars are hardly citing research from outside their own field. For what, for a sense of identity? Identity with what? Certainly not with truth and enlightenment but with a parochial mentality for a name and denomination.

Genuine dialogue is hardly present in scholarship. My experience and experience of my colleagues unequivocally indicate that most journal articles are not even ever read. I subscribe to 6 or 8 of the most prestigious journals in the field of communication. After reading the table of contents of each issue, they directly go to my bookshelf. They disillusion and appall me as to the condition of our scholarship.

National Communication Association's Annual Conference hardly represents scholarly dialog either. There are 3000 to 5000 scholars attending this conference every year. What actually happens is that all the hundreds of panels and groups are compartmentalized into hundreds of small rooms (or rather little cubicles). The mode of the number of audience members is 5-10. The Conference is certainly grand, but perhaps only so in its pomposity rather than in its effort to promote scholarly exchange. To be brutally frank and debunk the public secret, scholarship has become little more than an individualistic attempt to accumulate a larger and larger number of items on the resume. The focus has long been astray from cooperative exploration of the truth and implementation of the truth. I doubt that human genius can hatch anything else that is more wasteful than our current scholarship.

Scholarship is no longer clarifying and uniting, but departmentalizing and complicating. It has become a self-deceptive and self-accepted game of bibliography and numbers. It perhaps has perfect internal coherence, but it is no longer coherent with grave and urgent problems in the reality. Social sciences also need to shift its focus from studying phenomena to the studying of purpose and methods to fulfill the purpose. Existing phenomenon may be nothing but passive reflection of widespread social practices. Scholarship must become the center of light and the leader instead of a passive follower of existing reality. Scholarship must deal with what could be rather than what is. An attempt to deal only with the phenomena lead to departmentalization and hair-splitting analysis of details, which in turn lead to complication and confusion. Unification is simplification that represents an attempt to deal with the causes. Phenomena are many. Causes are few. This explains why a real theory has a small strong body but far-reaching tentacles. Our current scholarship rather feels like an anomalous octopus with too many tentacles but an emaciated body. Scholarship should not be an effort to make my case, but an effort to make our case. Truth in the component may be a crime in the whole. Striving for internal and logical coherence may lead us further astray from the coherence with the larger picture of purpose.

There is a big question for social sciences to solve. Why in so many fields of human endeavors, we know what we need to do, but yet we don't do it? More specifically, in the field of communication, students know what they need to do to better their communication, but they simply don't do it. What we need is no longer more knowledge and discoveries, but the implementation of the knowledge. The knowledge-action gap must be seriously addressed. The study of leadership may be another example. When we address what elements make great leadership, the answers become so obvious as to be campy. The question becomes, however, why we don't practice great leadership if we understand the ingredients of it? The knowledge-action gap must be addressed in many classrooms of social sciences.

2

The Dynamics of Human Attention

Human attention is limited, so that when it is engaged in the thing one loves, it excludes the external world and experiences the feeling of flow (or complete mental occupation). Children never get tired of play because they experience "flow." Tiredness is not a physical condition (too much work on the brain and body), but a psychological condition, conditioned by lack of an experiential flow.

If everyone experiences the "flow," perhaps social sciences, intended for solution of social problems, won't be much needed.

Human attention is volatile and has its own rhythm. Once scheduled and managed, it dies. The only way to nurture healthy and "flowing" human attention is to encourage voluntary and spontaneous *play*. Healthy humans only need to play and nothing else. Play should be for its own sake. Play is the root out of which we'll be able to get all that we really need. Creation is the natural product from play, not the purpose of play.

Human attention is limited and shifts. Our attention, devoid of external pressure, has its natural propensity to engage in changing creative activities. The psychological condition of "flow" we experience consequently can even compensate for physical needs that are not satisfied well. For instance, when you get too engrossed in reading, you may forget about your hunger for some time.

Any values other than joy from "flowingly" engaged attention dislocate and debilitate attention, which may be the root of "social problems." As Mark Twain said in *The Adventures of Tom Sawyer*, "Work consists of whatever a body is obligated to do, and play consists of whatever a body is not obligated to do." What influences or decides human attention shifts should rather be internal forces than external forces? An ideal society where the optimum economics is achieved is one where the majority of its denizens just play and savor the psychological experience of "flow."

Students' learning has its own rhythm. "Peak learning experience (PLE) is basically a unique experience for that human system at that particular moment. I am not discussing something which is nice or even educational manipulation. I am discussing the opportunity for human to learn in one's own way that is a prerequisite for coping, living, loving, giving and maturing" (Lippitt, 1981, p. 88).

The lives of adults as well as children go through phases that create key life transitions. These periods of transitions create anxiety, stress, challenge, coping needs, and the search process. During periods of role, life, or styles transition, learner readiness rhythm is in an optimal state for many people. The transition provides for "force" for learning (Levinson, 1978).

An ideal society where the optimum economics is achieved would be one where the majority of its denizens just play and savor the psychological experience of "flow."

References:

Levinson, D. (1978). The seasons of a man's life. New York: Knopf.

Lippitt, G. L. (1981). Learning as an opne system. In Lippitt, R. & Lippitt, G., (Eds.), Systems thinking—A resource for organization diagnosis and intervention. Washington, D. C.: International Consultants Foundation.

3

The Direction of Our Education

If we can claim that something gets wrong when most students don't enjoy their homework and lectures which constitute our education, then I'm afraid something really gets wrong with our education. I believe that education is not only a preparation for life, it should be life itself and a happy one. If this line of thinking is correct, it seems that something really needs to be changed.

What lies behind many students' boredom with lectures and homework is that they don't see voluntarily perceived values in their work and thus do not enjoy the work. Or we can say they are not doing things consciously out of their own will. Let's take the case of our childhood to show what constitutes "our own will." In our childhood, the more we played, the more we wanted to do it until we got physically tired. This activity of play may be considered an activity done with our own will. In adult life, we can also find such activity, like Edison's experimentation (It is said that he could do experiments for hours and hours). I believe Edison saw a strong value in his work and this perception of value offered him enjoyment of his work. So, what seems to constitute "our own will" are factors such as enjoyment and voluntarily perceived value in our work. The problem with our school education is that we judge students not by whether they can perceive, in their learning, joy and value which should be the real factors sustaining interest and motivation, but by whether and how well they have completed their homework. Shakespeare said, "To business that we love we rise betime, And return to it with delight." When students begin to enjoy, we'll have really industrious students.

Then how should we adjust or even transform our school system? From my reading of history, Cambridge used to employ the tutorial teaching method. The tutor will give the students projects or practical problems at the beginning of the semester and offers them guidance in reading. The students are supposed to read in the library on their own. Classes are available but not compulsory. In education thus designed, the students see a concrete value in their work with the problem ahead of them waiting for a solution. And what's more important is that the students don't feel pressure from constant homework and deadlines, which can make people frustrated, lazy, and constrained in developing further interests. When we work within a given and crowded schedule, we tend to narrow and lose our interests. When we lose interest, we lose enthusiasm and joy of life. It's fortunate that we don't need to take efforts to discover our interests. The natural curiosity for the unknown already gives more than enough interests for every newborn life. The matter is whether what we are doing is protecting the interests or destroying them. Not only is our current education damaging students' interests by making them follow the strict school schedule, our society is doing the same. Our society tells us that if you want to be successful by having money and titles, you have to concentrate on one thing (frequently a very narrow topic in a certain area of a certain discipline) and keep your eyes on that thing instead of peeping at things outside that thing road, even if those things are attractive as beautiful flowers.

J. T. Dillon offered us some ways to achieve happy education. I completely empathize with him and I'd like to make an effort to conduct my class in his direction. Whenever my students and I forget homework and discuss their real problems, and the connection between the problems and our learning, the students become interested, energetic and participative. The implications of Dillon's strategies are: Real education should free students from the terror of judgment, lead them to discover real values for their own life which contribute to a more harmonious and happy world, help them keep and nurture their interests in relation to realizing such a world, and teach them ways to substantiate their interests with practical work. We can hardly find a place for such an educational system in our present world, yet I believe the dream should be a direction rather than a location. We should readjust our practices so that we are walking toward our real wish instead of away from it. Although most students walk into colleges with the single purpose getting a degree, finding a good job with a good salary, this is not the purpose that the students voluntarily see for themselves. It is a forced condition. What they really want is an enjoyable and fruitful education for personal joy and growth. Yet people can no longer decide their purpose of going to college. Our grading system in education has inevitably focused students' attention on grades, credits, and finally a degree. The mode of education is competition rather than learning. Joy of learning has long been absent.

"There is no one villain to blame. There will be no magic pill. Significant change will require imagination, perseverance, dialogue, deep caring, and a willingness to change on the part of millions of people." Yet some of us have to start somewhere and now, so that one day people are judged not by what they have but by what they are (we are still not smart enough to know how to judge people by what they; it is much easier to judge people by looking at what they have), so that what people care is not the standard of *my living*, but the standard of *our life*. When this day comes, people will try to contribute rather than collect. And contributing leads to harmony and collecting leads to conflicts and even invasion. When this day comes, we derive our happiness not from others' envy of what we have accumulated, the process for which often produces toil and fatigue (not only for ourselves, but also for others), but from others' appreciation and memory of our work. All this depends on our shared perception of what is the real the purpose and value. And our education should give, more than anything else, this shared vision of the real value—the joy of our life. The first job of any evaluation must be first the clarification of the purpose, then the performance. Evaluation of performance without clarification of the purpose will inevitably leads to debilitating mediocrity and even destructive disaster.

4

Questions and Reflections on Students and Education

1. What is my dreamland?

I'm a radical dreamer, gazing most of the time at the ideal society. My "dreamland" is not a static place way out there in the distance, but rather the direction in which I lead my daily life. If we are moving away from competition which generates pressure and conflicts, and involuntary work which generates alienation and inactivity, and towards more enjoyment of our work which generates energy and hope, we are already in the "dreamland." But the unfortunate school reality is that most students hate classes and homework. And the unfortunate social reality is that countless people hate their jobs—and what tension and conflicts are evolving therein!

2. Is it true that everybody is yearning after his/her dreamland as defined above?

I can't say it is true for everybody, but my years of experience and personal interaction with people tell me that the majority of our fellows don't enjoy what they do as their jobs. If we can claim that if most people are not enjoying their jobs, something gets wrong, then something IS wrong, not only with our education but also with our system of work.

3. What constitutes "our own will"?

Let's take the case of the childhood. In our childhood, the more we played, the more we wanted to play until we got physically tired. This activity of play may be considered an activity done with our own will. In adult life, we can also find such activity, like Edison's experimentation (It is said that he could do experiments for dozens of hours on end). What seems to constitute "our own will" are factors like enjoyment and voluntarily perceived value in our work. The problem with our school education is that we judge students not by whether they can perceive in their learning joy and value which are the real factors sustaining interest and motivation, but by whether and how well they have completed their homework. Shakespeare said, "To business that we love we rise betime, And return to it with delight." When students begin to enjoy, we'll have really industrious students.

4. What's the meaning of "killing human nature"?

Human nature is what we see in children. For example, when children are small enough and not yet influenced by adult values, they don't judge people by their color, wealth, and the commonly understood "success." They judge people by their words and actions, their friendliness and so on. "Killing human nature" is the taking away of that part of human heart which combines us rather than divides us, which nurtures more interests and greater joy instead of more hatred of work.

5. How do we discover our interests? How are they developed in interaction with others?

We don't need to discover our interests. The natural curiosity for the unknown already gives more than enough interests for every newborn life. The matter is whether what we are doing is keeping the interests or killing them. The reality is that our interactions with others don't help keep but rather kill our interests bestowed to us by God, because people tend to judge you not by whether you have interests and enjoy your work and life, but by how successful you are on a basis of numerical comparison. Consequently, we then tend to lose more and more of our interests so that we can concentrate our efforts on a single activity which may make us "successful." Restraining and forcing one's attention on one activity gradually kills interests which change with our life.

6. Where do you position yourself in relation to J. T. Dillon's teaching strategies? What are the implications of such strategies? What educational system needs be in place in order to enact these strategies?

I completely empathize with J. T. Dillon and I'd like to make an effort to conduct my class in his direction. Whenever my students and I forget homework and discuss their real problems, the connection between the problems and our learning, the students become interested, energetic and participative. The implications of Dillon's strategies are: Real education should free students from the terror of judgment, lead them to discover real values for their lives that contribute to a more harmonious and happy world, help them keep and nurture their interests in relation to realizing such a world, and teach them ways to substantiate their interests with practical work.

We hardly find a place for such an educational system in our present world, yet as I said, the dream should be a direction of action rather than a location. We should modify our actions so that we walk toward our real wish instead of away from it. Unfortunately, the single purpose for most students' education now is a good job with a decent salary. And we know this is not the students' fault. Our whole value and evaluation system determines this and makes many of us feel quite often lost rather than directed. "There is no one villain to blame. There will be no magic pill. Significant change will require imagination, perseverance, dialogue, deep caring, and a willingness to change on the part of millions of people." Yet some of us have to start somewhere and now, so that one day people are judged not by what they have but by what they are, so that what people care is not the standard of *my living*, but the standard of *our life*, so that we can say we are all equal individuals no matter what, with the most important and noble pursuit of personal and communal happiness. When this day comes, people will try to contribute rather than collect. And contributing leads to harmony and collecting leads to conflicts and even invasion. When this day comes, we derive our happiness not from others' envy of our accumulating wealth, the process for which makes us toil and tire, but from others' appreciation and memory of our work. All this depends on our shared perception of what is the real value. And our education should give, more than anything else, this shared vision of the real value—the joy of our life.

5

The Organization of Education

Our organization of life depends on the organization of our institutions. The ideal organization of institutions should give us a feeling of flow where we have enough latitude and time to carry out our passionate interests to their completion. The end product then is one of sincerity and passion—one involving creativity and a sense of pride and fulfillment. The bad organization of institutions stops the fleeting impulses of inspiration, debilitates interests and passion and forces the attention to the scheduled tasks, many of which actually make little sense. In the bad organization of institutions, life is torn between what we want to do and what needs to be done on the one hand, and what actually is being done on the other hand.

Carrying out numerous tasks or, in the case of students, many courses concurrently without seeing a holistic pattern that threads them together kills energy. Our limited energy and attention make it very difficult for us to concentrate on many disconnected things at once. Consequently those courses that the student is not interested in not only divert their attention away from the ones they are interested in, but these courses also kill the time, energy, and passion by pressuring the student with the prospect of prospect of penalty in missing deadlines. Procrastination and indolence will become ubiquitous. The thinking is a wasteful folly that education depends on what we put the students through rather than what is left with them after the semester.

The development and growth of interests should not and cannot be planned. They should rather be nurtured. To nurture the interests, they have to be followed closely and continuously until their satisfaction. Diverting and restraining them for the sake of a myriad of other businesses destroy these interests. Interests, once planned, wilt.

Good schools should give students adequate intellectual sources rather than plan their time and interests. That is, if the student gets absorbed in a book, he will be able to read it till he feels tired, without worrying about going to the next class or about turning in the next paper in time. When people are absorbed in a topic, they'll naturally continue their reading in the topic; they'll naturally form ideas and make discoveries in the field; and they'll naturally produce honest scholarship. Planned schooling produces worry, pressure, boredom, and plagiarism. "Nurturing schooling" produces joy, love, real work, and honest scholarship. Schools should not make students "go down a little checklist in a mechanical, almost ritualistic sort of way" (Covey, 1993).

What our schools are doing now is not nurturing, but planning. They plan everything for the students, from class time to class contents, from homework to examinations, and from courses to departments. The list may be endless. If everything is planned, the students must progress in a pre-designed groove. This design has made it extremely difficult for lecturer to have the students' sustained attention; the mind simply doesn't work in that manner—you can't shift what you feel passionate about among five discrete things in a course of a day. The concept of progressing along a groove is against the concept of education that involves thinking and reflection, that espouses spontaneous initiative, exploration, discovery, and invention. I believe that if scientists put their attention only on the planned without noticing the unplanned, it will be tragic for them in terms of making great discoveries, because wonderful discoveries frequently come from the unplanned (The discovery of electro-magnetism is but one example of countless scientific "accidents".). Yet our schools are not learning lessons from great scientific experience. Our reality is that through reading and thinking, the student may suddenly find himself/herself passionate about one idea, but he/she can by no means pursue that idea because he/she has to go to another class and finish another paper during the rest of the day. It becomes an ongoing process of discovering interests and then kill them immediately just so that you can survive in the academic tunnel which is a one-way lane. The educational process for many students can be a constant struggle between what they want to do and what needs be done at the moment.

To realize the nurturing education, we must reorganize or redesign our present education. The whole education should be something like a fine library or information warehouse where the student has everything necessary. They go into the library or warehouse, read, think and discover. No time schedule to break their flow of interests and their spontaneity of exploration. If there is any director, it is not department syllabi or degree requirements, but their interests, passion, reading, thinking and newly discovered ideas. The teachers in a nurturing education are counselors rather than lecturers. They are living intellectual resources to complement the dead resources in the library. They are always available (not necessarily physically) for consultation, direction and correction needed by the students. In the nurturing school (a radical departure from what we have now), there are no departments, schedules or syllabi. However, there are recommended reading lists, summaries of literature in every discipline, and questions that represent possible additions to the present body of knowledge. All these are prepared and periodically updated by the teachers. The teachers' main job is to do research and act as living intellectual resources and counselors for students. The student should produce at least one substantive paper after their education. The paper should be able to solve or help some significant problem. The school degree-conferring committee decides whether the student can receive a degree by end of their years. If yes, which kind of degree, how many degrees, and which level of degree the student should receive based on their paper(s). So obviously, in this nurturing education, a portion of students may not be able to get degrees. Yet this nurturing school system focuses on learning and education instead of on schooling and acquisition of a degree. Thoughtful citizens rather than degreed zombies are produced. On the other hand, some students in the new system will obviously get multiple degrees and even degrees of masters and doctorates at the end of their four years. On the surface, the new system is creating a massive mess. Intrinsically, however, it is producing order and peace and quality unmatchable by the old system. More motivated students, more scholars and scientists will emerge more quickly.

Then there may come the worrying question of students' going astray if they follow only their own interests. I believe this will not happen, at least in the long run. In the nurturing school system, there will be enough honest interactions between students and books, among students themselves, between students and teachers and among teachers themselves. And honest interactions nurture the better nature and numb the devil-side within ourselves. Freedom to pursue happiness always produces a better and more civilized society, as historically proved. All the manifestations of the bad nature of humankind (cheating including plagiarism, backbiting, envy, discrimination, diffidence, etc.) are produced by forcing, pressure, and lack of honest interactions. When people can learn freely and voluntarily, they learn more and better. When people learn more and better, they become better individuals. The more such individuals we have, the better our world will be.

Reference:

Covey, S. R. (1993). <u>Spiritual roots of human relations</u>. Salt Lake City, UT: Deseret Book Company.

6

Motivation in Learning

"There are a thousand hacking at the branches of evil to one who is striking at the root" (Henry David Thoreau). Lack of motivation lies at the root of our educational problems. When people are really motivated, they begin to genuinely care and they are naturally committed. They are doing what they truly want to do. They are full of energy and enthusiasm. They persevere, even in the face of frustration and setbacks, because what they are doing is *their* work. The most important ingredient in learning/teaching is the motive, the *horme*, or the purpose driven energy (Covey, 1993). Depending on different motives or motivation, people can learn better in prison than in a fine classroom, and the former can even *feel* better than the latter. My personal experience with countless people inform me so. Covey believes that unless the learner is involved and dynamically participates in the learning process, very little, if any, learning (changed behavior) will result.

If we compare students to a radio. Motivation should be the switch. And teaching techniques are like the tuning knobs. If the switch is not turned on, fumbling with the tuning knobs in whatever manner won't produce any result. Learning comes first not from the teacher, but from the learner.

What is our reality? According to Raffini (1993), large numbers of students are rejecting schools as a means for improving their lives. They come to school simply because they have to. Schooling and education have become mechanical business-like procedures to trudge through by zombie-like students. This has become but another senseless ritual of life to pass.

There are two kinds of motivation: intrinsic and extrinsic, and they are different in nature. Simply stated, an intrinsically motivating activity is one in which there is no apparent or compelling reason for doing the activity, beyond the satisfaction derived from the activity itself. Psychologist Mihaly Csikszentmihalyi from the University of Chicago believes the subjective feelings of pleasure and enjoyment are the intrinsic rewards that cause people to perform certain activities. He uses the term *flow* to describe the phenomenon in which individuals become so completely absorbed with a task that they are unaware of the passage of time and the location of their physical space. When a person experiences flow, according to Csikszentmihalyi, "he or she will experience a contraction of the perceptual field, a heightened concentration on the task at hand, a feeling of control leading to elation and finally to a loss of self awareness that sometimes resets in a feeling of transcendence, or a merging with the activity and environment."

According to Raffini, four factors contribute to Intrinsic Motivation: a. challenge: b. curiosity; c. control; d. fantasy (which can arouse imagination). Our current educational system, especially its evaluation or grading system, is destroying the remnants of students' intrinsic motivation (Reeve and Deming).

There lack congruence of values among teachers, students, family, and society. Generative learning occurs only when people are striving to accomplish something that matters deeply to themselves, something that betters human condition over time. A task not consistent with values that people live by day by day will not only fail to inspire genuine enthusiasm, it will often foster outright cynicism. We must work at learning how to separate what we truly want, from what we think need to be done in order to achieve it. The means and the end are too often confused.

Competition is destroying students' needs for (1) self-worth; (2) autonomy and self-determination; and (3) belong and relatedness. Most students are forced to choose between the paths of academic apathy or academic competence as the route to follow through the daily routine of school life. Education is nowhere to be found.

"Stickers, candy, grades, prizes, deadlines, surveillance, and other incentives are ubiquitous in the classroom. As teachers and parents subject students to a constant barrage of external contingencies, students naturally adapt to the demands of the school culture. In their adaptation, however, students take on a greater extrinsic motivational orientation by focusing increasingly less on the process of learning and increasingly more on its products—grades, evaluations, jobs, scholarships, approval, and the like. Gradually students experience an ever-growing increase in their academic extrinsic motivation and, therefore, an ever-diminishing developmental decline in their academic intrinsic motivation. With each advancing grade, students perceive that school becomes more impression, more forma, more evaluative, more competitive, and basically less intrinsically motivating."

If we don't motivate students with things like grades and degrees, will students become lazy and inactive learners? Deci & Ryan (pp. 32-33): "The intrinsic needs for competence and self-determination motivate an ongoing process of seeking and attempting to conquer optimal challenges. When people are free from the intrusion of drives and emotions, they seek situations that interest them and require the use of their creativity and resourcefulness. They seek challenges that are suited to their competencies, that are neither too easy nor too difficult…In short, the needs for competence and self-determination keep people involved in ongoing cycles of seeking and conquering optimal challenges."

References

Ball, S. (Ed.). (1977). <u>Motivation in education</u>. New York: Academic Press.

Covey, S. R. (1993). <u>Spiritual roots of human relations</u>. Salt Lake City, UT: Deseret Book Company.

Deming, W.E. (1986). <u>Out of the crisis</u>. Cambridge, MA: Massachussets Institute of Technology, Center for Advanced Engineering Study.

Deming, W.E. (1993). <u>The new economics</u>. Cambridge, MA: Massachussets Institute of Technology, Center for Advanced Engineering Study.

Deci, E. & Ryan, R. (1985). <u>Intrinsic motivation and self determination in human behavior</u>. New York: Phenum Press.

Hesselbein, F., Goldsmith, M. & Beckhard, R. (Eds.) (1996). <u>The leader of the future</u>. San Francisco: Jossey-Bass.

Nicholls, J. G. (1989). <u>The competitive ethos and democratic education</u>. Cambridge, MA: Harvard University Press.

Raffini, J. P. (1993). Winners without losers: <u>Structures and Strategies for increasing student motivation to learn</u>. Needham Heights, MA: Allyn & Bacon.

Reeve, J. (1996). <u>Motivating others: Nurturing inner motivational resources</u>. Needham Heights, MA: Allyn & Bacon.

Wlodkowski, R. J. & Jaynes, J. H. (1990). <u>Eager to learn: Helping children become motivated and love learning</u>. San Francisco: Jossey-Bass.

7

The Mission of the University

To be a college student and then a college professor have long been my dream, because the university for me is the most promising place where I can lead, not a living, but a life. But I have become disillusioned with what is happening in many of our universities.

I love my undergraduate years, because they were years of growth for me, growth of my body, growth of my mind, and growth of understanding and life. I devoured books like a hungry wolf, because I found beauty, dream, and promise in the books I read. Every night I longed for the daybreak. Sleeping was half death for me, because it is, most of the time, an inanimate numbness. In sleep I lost so much which I could enjoy doing in the daytime. I believed people live in three states: life, death, and pain. Life is active love, joy and voluntary work; death is numbness, a lack of feeling and thinking; pain, it seems at present time, is forced effort for survival. Life is the best state; death is the second; pain is the worst. What the university should do is to uplift its students so that they live more in the first state, the state of life.

Unfortunately, countless universities are not doing the desired work to enable their students to live a life of joy and learning. The focus is on "making a living" rather than on "leading a life." Our universities largely make the majority of their students worry about grades, which in turn represents a worry about the degree, which in turn represents a worry about the job, which in turn represents the worry about survival. Thus, if the university puts the students into perpetual worry, it puts the students into perpetual pain, which is a worse state than death. I believe few college students nowadays, in order to read and write more, long for the coming daybreak. They long for the holiday break instead. This also holds true for most of our citizens, the product of our schools. All this testifies, at least to a certain degree, to a failure of our schools, particularly of our universities.

In a talk with a student who received education from probably the best Chinese university, I learned his belief that the society should be ruled by the small group of elite, entitled to an over-wealth by their "intelligence and industry;" that the multitude should be kept in poverty and inequality, so that they are always aware of their need to overcome their stupidity and indolence; that civilization is represented by a continuous materialistic satisfaction of the continuously developing needs of the elite; that for this satisfaction, it is justified to treat the multitude, whose emotions are a big drag on progress, as running cogs of the managerial mega-machine. He especially emphasized the necessity of a vast inequality to the masses because of their "bad human nature." His philosophy is that the masses should be put under a high-handed ruling mechanism which treats them as "things of motions" rather than "persons of acts." After hearing all this, I became so angry, not so much against the student, as against the failure of our higher education. The insensibility that is still so clear in many of our educated! When it strikes me that this Chinese student's belief is harbored by many of the best educated I have encountered in person or through reading, I suddenly see images of poverty, slavery, despotism, greed, war, general human misery, and, most of all, the horror of rotting human spirit.

Our scholars, on the other hand, are not uniting their voices against the most obvious and widespread pain or problems in our life. Few talk about the obvious and general problems. They do research mainly in light of publications for tenure and promotion. I consider many of our prolific scholars as the best pettifoggers who have mastered, through long years of writing, the ability to talk voluminously about the most arcane and insignificant without actually saying much. Much scholarship could be considered as packages of petty discoveries wrapped in the super-thick, recycled paper of arcane language.

There is also a very bad tendency in social sciences and humanities. Scholars in these fields tend to follow the norm of natural sciences and believe numbers are much more valid proof and evidence than widespread acute feelings and sentiments. This is probably why Covey (1993) claimed that sentiment rather than logic often is wisdom. Many of our scholars spend enormous amount of time numerically substantiating the most widespread and self-evident human feelings. Or worse, they collect data in expedient manners for quick publications and then present conclusions based on such data as valid discoveries. Just look how many statistical studies are based on university classroom students only (because of convenience of such populations) and then present themselves as study of the general society.

The mentality of statistics has become so much ingrained in our scholars' minds that they would rather choose to believe whatever the experts' numerical research tells them rather than the most self-evident supported by history and popular experience. To prove this, Neil Postman (1993) did an experiment. One morning he told his fellow professors that the *New York Times* just had published an article about a discovery by some famous physiologists from John Hopkins University. These experts discovered a strong connection between jogging and deterioration of mental power. Most of the professors believed what he said (Neil Postman, 1993). What an illustrating experiment. We are allowing ourselves to be constantly confused by incoherent and fragmented "discoveries" which are based on expedient and inaccurate statistical data. The confusing incoherence in various conclusions may well derive from the fact that different studies are based on tiny slices of reality instead the reality itself but claim themselves as studies of the reality. The end product of such scholarship can easily lead to agnosticism, which may eventually emaciate human ideals and purposes. Many of our scholars are becoming mere logic processors and manipulators without a coherent and significant subject matter. They manufacture products called "conclusions and discoveries" by processing whatever bits of information that happens to fall into their hands. The chaotically flowing and expanding sea of information and discoveries in social sciences and humanities do not help put us on a better track toward wherever we really want to go.

Very rarely do I come across a journal article that makes me excited, optimistic, joyful, and long for genuine betterment of the life condition of my own and of my fellows. The more journal articles I read, the more I find myself asking, "How can I master the academic art of writing copiously and logically about the tiny corner of the un-researched so that I can get published too? I should forget about whether the study is significant or coherent with constant human sentiments." We have investigation estimating that, of all the articles in even the most prestigious scholarly journals, "less than half were ever read by anyone, that less than one-fifth were cited more than once" (Van Patten, 1996, p.50). What a human cost and loss! How many of our best scholars put their prime years in such publications! Many scholars of humanities and social sciences have forgotten that their job should be to see that the ladder of life is against the right wall, whereas the job of natural scientists may be to see that we are climbing this ladder more efficiently. It may not be a good thing for humanities and social sciences to engage in a rat race for more "discoveries." We will not become anything more than rats even if we win in a rat race. Perhaps we should slow down our "discoveries" and unite our voices to enhance the unifying and motivating human spirit. Otherwise the bitter valley between what we see and what we genuinely espouse will continue to devour us into its widening mouth. There should exist a check and balance between natural sciences on the one hand and humanities and social sciences on the other hand so that we gradually narrow the gap between societal rationality and reality and individual rationality and reality, so that we progress on the secure highway balanced between materialist heedlessness and traditionalist caution. However advanced a society, its big societal life has to be lived through its individual citizens' lives. Without a proper mechanism of check and balance, "social development," under whatever gaudy disguises, will remain despotism in nature as far as the life experience of individual citizens is concerned.

Free pursuit of knowledge, advocated by our higher education, should be sincerely after what we truly believe can better human life. This pursuit should not be for the academic degree or professional tenure, which are mere byproducts from the pursuit. The pursuit should be a matter of mission, conscience, nobility, joy, and destiny. It is very hard to see sincerity and conscience now in the designing of our universities and their courses. What rules again are statistics, numbers and quotas. We no longer care much about whether our education uplifts the students so that they live more in the state of life instead of in the state of "death" and pain. We more care about whether they have completed a certain number of papers with a certain number of pages, which usually translate into fulfillment of a certain number of credits. We no longer care much about whether our professors inspire the students to live and work more; we more care about whether they fulfill a certain number of publications and credit hours of teaching. In other words, our higher education administrators care more about evidence that is easily quantifiable, which is not necessarily evidence of real effectiveness. This may only reflect the indolence of our administrators because numerical evidence after all is a much easier instrument to wield when it comes to evaluation and accountability.

In addition, accountability through numbers and quotas underlie mistrust, between the administrators and the professors, between the professors and the students, between the universities and the general public. The underlying implication is clearly that, "How can I believe you are working if I do not see you have done a certain number of things?" Life with mistrust as its underlying assumption only breeds more mistrust. The consequent race of numbers also breads and encourages less attention to quality and the practice of dishonesty such as plagiarism. When numbers and quotas get to control people's lives, people will remain disillusioned in a secret and debilitating sense of failure, because no one ultimately can win a race with numbers. A number of 10 publications is certainly a loser to that of 20, which in turn is certainly a loser to that of 40. This can go on and on. The only way to survive in this environment is either get by with the least effort which ideally reflects itself in the greatest number of products with the least acceptable quality, or beat oneself up with a numb diligence, justified by "survival."

Free pursuit of knowledge means that the only schedule for the scholar is her reading and thinking, at her own pace. Wherever her reading, thinking and experimenting (with a sincere wish for a better *human* condition) takes her, she simply follows. Other forms of externally imposed schedules interfere with and compromise the emergence of true knowledge. This is probably why Lippitt says that learning has its own rhythm, "Peak learning experience (PLE) is basically a unique experience for that human system at that particular moment. I am not discussing something which is nice or even educational manipulation. I am discussing the opportunity for human to learn in one's own way that is a prerequisite for coping, living, loving, giving and maturing" (Lippitt, 1981, p. 88).

Currently, the externally imposed schedules are reflected in course calendars, office hours, course offerings in a certain semester, and a certain number of assignments in a specific course which may not have a central theme among them. Consequently the university largely means, for the student, a place for accumulating enough credits in a limited time. However, time wasted because of students' apathy in classrooms and assignments is ignored. Textbooks swallowed or rather purchased and unread without much digestion is ignored. Pages and pages written without much sincere consciousness are acquiesced. The terminus of scholarship may have become the printing of words in a nice-looking format, presentable as another item in the resume. The popular inner voice of thousands repeatedly calling for basic changes is suppressed, withered, and killed by the simple fact of life that, to survive, you have to be so busy in the race of numbers that you have little mental power left for reflection and construction. We schedule everything so neatly that we forget that the creative and productive human spirit simply cannot be scheduled. The only way to nurture and grow it is for it to follow its own course and passion. The genuinely effective education provides an environment for the nurturing and growing of the human spirit.

John Henry ("Cardinal Newman," an Oxford graduate) spoke of the University as a place of perpetual residence, intellectually and spiritually, if not always physically, even unto death (Shi, 1987, p. 164). Our students, however, want to get out of the university as quickly as possible. And professors have unfortunately taken this as the only natural student mentality. Education to countless students is but a necessary and required evil. When more and more territory in our life becomes a necessary and required evil, we fall into the worse-than-death desert of fatalism, pessimism, depression, and soul-eating languor. It is hard to say that students' life is not a pain when it is constituted by constant have-to-do'es instead of motivating passions. This is a serious question for our higher education and our scholars to think about and tackle, not only for the sake of students' life, but for the sake of everyone else's life. Yet we usually retreat at the slightest hint of this question. Our indolence dissuades us from the endeavor to discover and design methods to evaluate on the basis of genuine evidence rather than easy evidence.

John Henry Newman gave a series of speeches upon establishing Dublin Catholic University. The title of the speech series is "The Ideal of a University." In these speeches he emphasized the idea of free pursuit of knowledge. His ideal university is the original Oxford type, a university "which had no professors or examinations at all, but merely brought a number of young men [women] together for three or four years, and then sent them away" (Shi, 1987, p. 164). This surely sounds too radical now, but we clearly see the underlying philosophy. Newman's philosophy goes against a strict schedule in higher education, which exacts "of its members an acquaintance with every science under the sun." When a university attempts to achieve this, it only makes most of its students busy, demotivated, and then indolent. Actually when we try to exact from the students an acquaintance with every necessary science by offering them a well-rounded spectrum of courses, our patchwork in courses tends to make them lose sight of connections which make up the whole picture of human purpose; we tend to slowly but surely nudge our students out of their avid interests. Understanding of connections within the holistic human purpose only comes from deep, honest, voluntary, and sustained study. Such a study of any significant field will naturally lead the student into exploring many other fields, because he will realize on his won, rather than being told by others, that he cannot possibly keep up with his pursuit of any knowledge without going into various disciplines. Only through engagement in deep and voluntary study will the student find the connected view of our problems, will she see the actual mechanism that mysteriously produces our problems and thus acquire enough optimism, energy, and design to solve the problems. Otherwise, the student will see no whole and no center and will easily get cynical and disillusioned.

Many consider the University merely as a forced *preparation* for a decent life. I believe that the university period should not only be good life itself, but also the best life, because during this period, we are actually studying how to live the best possible life by pondering about human purpose and trying to solve human problems. If life cannot be the best during this period, when can it be? This is perhaps why the very first part of the Objective Statement of Southern Illinois University is "to exalt beauty in God, in Nature, and in Art" (as seen on the wall of the University's library). The ability to see beauty is certainly an important component of a good life. Thus speaking, for instance, if the student cannot find "tongues in the trees, books in the running brooks" (Shakespeare), our education can be considered a failure. Thus speaking, a successful university makes its students want to stay, not for the final degree, but for the joy, the enlargement and cultivation of the mind that her every day in the university can offer. This is also why I am often nostalgic about my undergraduate years when I was blessed with enough time to cultivate space and capabilities in my mind to see beauty in nature, in poetry, in love; when I was able to find so much joy from every present moment in every present day; when my only agenda was to read, think, and interact, out of which emerged some grand dream for human life. After further progress in life, I realized, to my greatest dismay, that my life was sliced into busy, disconnected and insignificant pieces in the name of efficiency.

For free pursuit of knowledge, the only feasible schedule for higher education is perhaps the student's natural curiosity and wish for joy, beauty, knowledge, and an urge for her fulfillment. Whenever I leisurely browse through a good library, I find so much to enjoy, to learn, to be encouraged by, and to be occupied with. At such moments, I always become oblivious of time and space, and feel motivated to work more and to contribute more to the general society as the great people around our life did or are doing. This phenomenon is perhaps what psychologists call the "flow." If everybody's every day is a "flow," we have the best citizens and thus the best society. Pre-scheduling is perhaps the biggest enemy to such a "flow" because the natural human curiosity and wish to learn is free-flowing in nature. This is perhaps why John Henry Newman advocated his ideal university with no professors and examinations, but with a fine library. I believe following the direction from the soul gives joy, spontaneity, creation, and accomplishment, all of which tend to be jeopardized by too much scheduling. A great college life is not so much planned as lived, not so much disciplined as motivated, not so much taught as learned. The final purpose of education is the bringing-forth of the human essence in the soul of the student or the installation of character into the student, as the old mission of the Harvard University claimed. Once this is achieved, everything else is basically achieved. Once this fails, everything else remains basically futile, because the human essence in the soul is the fountainhead of virtue, freedom, responsibility, understanding, and wisdom. The human essence reminds and liberates us by keeping us on our guard against all despotism clothed in racism, improper administration, sexism, fake science and technology, and other forms which may still be unknown to us. Too much scheduling and numerical quota defertilize the soil in the student's soul where the true human essence grows, thrives, and spreads.

Therefore, I believe good schools should provide students with adequate intellectual sources rather than plan their time and interests. That is to say, when the student gets absorbed in a book, he has the freedom to read it till he feels tired, without worrying about going to the next class or finishing the next due paper. When people are absorbed in a topic, they will naturally continue their reading in the topic; they will naturally form ideas and make discoveries in the field; and they will naturally produce honest scholarship. Scheduled schooling based on numerical evidence and accountability produces worry, pressure, boredom, and prolific publications that are never read. "Nurturing schooling" produces joy, love, honest scholarship, and significant work. Higher education will fail miserably if it forces students "down a little checklist in a mechanical, almost ritualistic sort of way" (Covey, 1993).

When the student has to progress in a pre-designed groove, creativity and discovery, which is the essence of scholarship, are largely doomed. Our current design of higher education makes it very difficult for lecturers to have the students' constant attention, because all the fragmentations in our educational system do not reward and constantly debilitate sustained attention and effort. The concept of progressing along a groove is absolutely against the concept of education and scholarship, which derive their life from spontaneous initiative and intrinsic motivation. To illustrate, the student, when reading and thinking, may suddenly find himself passionate about this idea, but he has to finish the homework concerning another topic. Along the way of education, the student may find herself passionate about a new discipline, but she fears being bogged down by the undesirable consequences if she diverges into the new discipline. The educational process for many students can be a debilitating struggle between what they want to do and what needs be done at the moment.

To realize the concept of nurturing education, we need to reorganize or redesign our education. Higher education should be something like a fine library. The student has all necessary resources there. They enter the university and read, think, interact, and discover. No time schedule should break their flow of interests and work of exploration. If there is any director, it is not department syllabi or degree requirements, but human problems and their interests, passion, reading, thinking, and newly discovered ideas. The teachers in the nurturing education are mentors rather than lecturers. They are living intellectual resources to complement the passive resources in the library. They are always available (not necessarily physically) for consultation, guidance, and assistance when needed by the students. In this nurturing school, which is certainly a radical departure from what we have become so obdurate with, there are no departments, schedules, or syllabi. There may be reading lists, summaries of research literature, questions that may incite new additions to the present body of knowledge, and, perhaps most importantly, free interaction among all professors and students in their mutual intellectual growth. Professors may update the reading lists and research reviews. Yet their main job is to interact and research collaboratively with the student(s). The student should produce at least one substantive paper after their stay in the university. The paper should be able to help solve some significant human problem. Collaborative papers may be acceptable. The school degree conferring committee, composed of professors in all schools of thought and science, decides whether the student can receive a degree upon the time of graduation. If yes, the committee should determine which kind of degree, which level of the degree, and how many degrees the student should receive. This manner of education may look slow in process, but will be drastically better in results. I believe effective education should be like the progress of moon, perceptible not in progress, but in results, not as a storm that does not get much water into the ground, but as the drizzle that moistens the depth of the ground.

Effective education will enable the students to become, upon graduation, degree-holders in name, but useful citizens and even geniuses in character.

References:

Covey, S. R. (1993). Spiritual roots of human relations. Salt Lake City, UT: Deseret Book Company.

Henry, J. (1987). The ideal of a University. In Y. S. Shi (Trans.), One hundred famous speeches. Beijing, China: China Foreign Translation Publishing Company.

Lippitt, G. L. (1981). Learning as an open system. In Lippitt, R. & Lippitt, G., (Eds.), Systems thinking—A resource for organization diagnosis and intervention. Washington, D. C.: International Consultants Foundation.

Postman, N. (1993). Technopoly: The surrender of culture to technology. New York: Vintage.

Van Patten, J. J. (1996). The culture of higher education: A case study approach. Lanham, MD: University Press of America.

8

The Sense of Home and the Personal Classroom

Rumi, a 13th century Persian poet once wrote:

> Out beyond ideas of rightdoing and wrongdoing
> There is a field
> I will meet you there
> When the soul lies down in that grass
> The world is too full to talk about

This poem I once used to describe the relationship between me and my wife. For many times, we are together without speaking a word to each other. But we both understand that this silence is not the frightening void, but the precious and peaceful sense of fullness or home where our most natural selves dwell. Home is the place to which we can always retreat and be natural.

I find this "sense of home" precious because I don't have it in so many things I do. I mean I am at odds with myself in so many of my daily engagements. I continually ask myself questions like: "Where am I going?" "Where should I go?" "What and where is the work in which I may entrust my whole life and find continuous and renewed joy and peace so that I no longer have to change, shift, adapt, control, manipulate, and struggle; so that I can be settled and just be?" How wonderful it is to feel settled and enjoy the bit of work we love, as D. H. Lawrence said, "In an ideal society, everybody can find the bit of work that he enjoys."

I sometimes admire monks. Although their temple may appear small, their life can nevertheless reach so far that their seemingly monotonous engagement in their physical world is no longer frightening as is in the secular eye, but can be so enriching as to sustain and support them till the very end of their physical life.

Only two kinds of hearts can do this, one that is completely dead and one that is completely conscious and alive. I believe some monks are really of the latter case. Someone said that the happiest person is one who can connect the beginning of his life with the ending of his life—by the single engagement that offers sustained joy.

The real personal classroom or education should make the student a doer and lover instead of a shifter and struggler. It should help the student find the "sense of home." Once this is in place, the students will be able to soar with the wings of curiosity, intelligence, and creativity. Time and schedule no longer matters when we address ourselves to things we value and love.

PART III

Society and Life

1

Life, Turning Points in Life, and Suicide

I have learned one thing from my life of 35 years old (Whew, I can't believe I'm already 35, but if I can live till 85, I still have another half century to live): Things generally turn out to be better than what I initially imagine and worry about. This is more true to people who often find themselves thinking about and give attention to their future. Turning points (such as college graduation) in life can be moments of uncertainty and emotional turbulence. Yet turning points in our life are also moments of choices, new designs, new roads, and new hopes. To protect ourselves and preserve our energy and even life, we need to perceive every turning point in life as such. This perception is not whimsical or self-deceptive, but largely represents reality. Countless people emerge as great successes from the nadir of poverty or despair because such moments in life offer opportunities for serious reflection and new choices. All the great presidents of the U.S. emerged so because of large-scale crises and conflicts (e.g., the Independence War, the Civil War, the Depression, and the WWII). A life always in an established rut rarely produces grandeur and memory.

It is sad to learn about suicides every day everywhere in the world, even in the best and most romantic season of the year like the spring. Spring is so beautiful in this earthly world that I just want to linger a little longer. It is very dangerous to look at life just from one perspective—you can get stuck in the abysmal well of despair and do actions because of the flash of a fleeting impulse. The consequences from such actions are frequently irretrievable and permanent, such as suicide and murder. I frequently try to reflect upon my life from different perspectives of all the possible vicissitudes that could have happened in my life every day. What if I failed to enter a college? What if I lost my legs in an accident? What if I became blind? What if I didn't come the States? Such things happen to thousands of people nonstop every day. Certainly most of them are not killing themselves just because their present life is not in conformity with whatever whimsical design they happen to have for their life at that moment.

I tell my students that the scope of human perception is extremely confined. For instance, we are human and we have just two eyes that can only look in one direction to a certain distance at any moment. Despite modern transportation and great mobility, most people's life experience is still confined to one region in their country. Because of the limited scope of human attention and perception, we never get to see the totality of even our individual life at any moment. What we see at a certain moment is but a tiny slice of that life. If you look at the seamy side of your life, your life immediately becomes gloomy. If you look at the sunny side of your life, it immediately becomes jolly. Many people, unfortunately, do not seem to understand that everyone's life is a fair share of the "sunlight" which is a prismatic combination of the seven colors. Some people only seem to focus on the dark colors and see their life as nothing but darkness. It thus becomes critically important where you focus your eyes in your life because our perception is humanly limited and we can impossibly intake the totality of our individual life. The focus of perception becomes especially important if we become aware of the fact that any life has to be lived through the spontaneous flow of experience rather than for the final terminus of something. In the former case, life is lived in its natural form of life; in the latter case, life is lived in misery in hopeful exchange for some elusive futurity. Every life can be lived either as life or as misery. The drastic difference may just come from a slight shift in perspective. Try shifting the eye-piece of the telescope just a tiny bit, what you see then will be dramatically altered.

I often think and tend to be convinced that there is no other purpose in life than the rational and conscious pursuit of joy and happiness. This purpose prompts us to actively employ our mind, heart, and hands to engage in something that is exciting. Sitting there doing nothing or sleeping in bed is in itself no fun at all unless the only other choice is imposed work which naturally becomes pain. Material acquisitions, money, fame, success, recognition, and all the other earthly trinkets should only be considered as the "by-products" from the pursuit of joy. All of these, unfortunately, are perceived millions as the primary motivators of life. The societal system of reward and penalty everywhere, tragically, is also based on such trinkets. Ineluctable epidemics such as indolence, procrastination, nonchalance, boredom, ennui, envy, hauteur, humiliation, prejudice, stress, and pessimism become ubiquitous. Work, the most important liberator of our mind and body, has become the source of pain to countless people, simply because of our tragic manner in which work is evaluated and approached. Since most of us have to work 40 hours a week, pain inescapably becomes the main ingredient in life. For one instance, the fog of boredom has engulfed the majority of college classrooms and business offices. Our current reward and promotion system, at its best, produces an economy of sub-optimization. The best and optimum economy can only be achieved when joy, creativity, and an urgent sense of purpose and fulfillment becomes the motivator of human work. In the optimum economy, leadership becomes easy, productivity becomes high, quality is assured, and, most importantly, work becomes joyful.

I believe that the only life worth living is the one that is propelled by a planed, somber, and single-minded pursuit of joy, real joy defined in a rationally educated manner (Some confuse joy with drunkenness or myopic addiction). Life could be lived and experienced in several forms: pain, death, numbness, and joy. The worst is pain. The next worst is death (This is probably why some choose suicide over pain). The next worst is numbness (This is why many prefer to drink, to drug, and to sleep—all to achieve a sense of numbness that is better than pain and death). The best and natural form is life. Only the minority are spending their waking hours in the form of life. The majority of us drag along in our waking hours, not living a life, but making a living. In life, one can't wait for the new day to come; one can't wait to engage in further work since it is liberating and edifying. In life, the momentum points forward where schedule and space no longer matter. In living, the momentum points backward or sideways. Just look how many students prefer sleep over classroom, and procrastination over an early completion of their work.

When joy becomes easily achievable, the leader does not need the whip to constantly goad people. You actually can't stop people from going forward and doing more. What else can't beat an economy propelled by such momentum? The pursuit of joy, when it becomes achievable, necessitates the constant engagement of hands, minds, and hearts.

Currently, most employees are only employed with their hands and heels, but rarely with their hearts and minds which stop functioning when the feet cross the office doorstep. Employment only with hands and heals is an incalculably prodigious waste in modern economy, so much so that thousands and thousands can't even eke out a mere livelihood working 60 hours a week. I can't find any other tyrannical insult against human intelligence and industry.

Our world now is exactly one of "zombies," with most of its members living in debilitating and lackadaisical ennui and boredom or even pain. Ubiquitous procrastination is but one indicator. The biggest tragedy against humanity is yet to be defined. It is not war, not poverty, not disease, not terrorism, all of which are but the superficial manifestations of the primal tragedy of all—our irrational organization and design of work, and our insensible system of reward and penalty.

2

Individual Needs and Group Goals

We should depart from individual needs. Why? One, we perceive our world through the lens of personal needs and problems. However far we have gone on our journey of life, we started there. Two, individual needs should be our north star because the individual needs we are born with are few and similar with those of others.

Our needs now are many, varied, and complicated. This situation is caused by our ways of interactions with each other, which have created an elaborate and yet frequently insensible system. Do you need to smoke? No. You do it because others do it and an external value is attached to it (e.g., the peer perception of being cool). Do you need to be successful by beating others? No. We do it because we are shown or told that it makes us great. Do we need to work 40 or even 60 hours a week to make a living? No. Our definition of life, design of work, and the system of rewarding have made us to do so. Does it make sense to put metal hooks into your back and have helicopters lift you up? No. You are persuaded that this will make you famous, which, you are told, is good. Many things in our life never made any sense if they are reflected through the lens of our primate and important individual needs. Yet, through group interactions and imitation, humans have the genius to make the most insensible become acceptable and ubiquitous social practices.

The great majority of the public perceive their organization from their personal problems and goals. If they can't see a connection, direct or indirect, between their personal needs and aspirations and the organizational goal and practice, they won't feel much voluntary motivation to carry out the organizational goal. Real leadership must be able to clearly show and strengthen this connection, no matter how intricate this connection may appear. The next step for the leader is to help the led transcend their personal problems and concerns to fulfill the organizational goal. It makes easy sense to any sensible mind that individuals now cannot maintain their joy and wealth if the surrounding world is one of misery and poverty, and that the real solution of many of our personal problems lies in the solution of the systemic problem. This is why many self-improvement programs are short-lived if our world is still one of unreason and falsity.

Unfortunately, a connection between individual needs and goals and organizational needs and goals is nowhere to be found in countless modern organizations. This is why practice of effective leadership has become so rare, even though everyone understands the ingredients of effective leadership.

Social scientists should make it their major task to shorten the distance between individuals' personal needs and goals and the group's needs and goals. This distance is in negative proportion to the degree of civilization of a group. The longer that distance, the less civilized that group is. This job for social scientists can only be achieved by studying, modifying, and even transforming our systemic ways of doing things. For a society with lasting prosperity and peace, group practices should follow out of the primate and most important individual needs. The most important part of the U.S. Constitution is based on this thinking.

We now seem to have a confusing and uncontrollable myriad of individual needs. This is not because we are born so, but because we have been so long victims of arbitrary and insensible group needs and valuation systems. The bulk of our current individual needs are not inherent, but created and conditioned by insensible group needs and goals forced on the individual.

The remedy now lies in greater patience and tolerance of the system toward the individual. Initially, there may be some confusion from conflicts among different socially conditioned needs in the individuals. Yet gradually, the system's tolerance and patience with the individual will accelerate the individual's discovery of his/her inherent and primate needs. When the majority of the individuals in the group have achieved this, they will find that they are after all all the same. When this is achieved, formulation and implementation of group goals, and hence leadership, becomes as easy as natural birth. It is simply the reification of the voice of any one in the group since they all have a coherent voice.

For a better and quicker remedy to social problems, the system needs to be one of such tolerant diversity that it becomes able to accommodate current individual values. Accommodation instead of imposition is better persuasion that influences the individual to freely pursue his/her pure, uncontaminated needs and wishes, which are the best safety valve for the group peace.

I deeply believe that a group based on pure, uncontaminated individual needs and wishes (which are few and homogenous) will be a harmonious one with lasting peace and joy. When the system treats the individual with empathy and patience, and when the individual is given freedom to travel the journey to reach their home where lies their pure, uncontaminated needs and wishes, this individual will be the first to realize the importance of empathy and tolerance; this individual will be the first to see that the only joy in life and in a social group, is the conscious pursuit of somber joy. The unconscious pursuit of morbid joys abounds in our society simply because the system is not treating the individual with empathy and patience, and the individual is not given freedom to travel the journey to reach their home where lies their pure, uncontaminated needs and wishes.

3

Religion as Remedy to Social and Individual Problems

I am still a freethinker and do not solidly belong to any religion, although I read the Christian Bible occasionally. As I understand, religion largely changes people's attitude toward or perception of reality. Religion to many people only provides a comfortable island to rest in the sea of realistic troubles. Religion to many is not used an instrument to change the seas of realistic troubles and problems. The more we retreat into a tiny zone of personal comfort in one corner of our heart, the more the insensible social practices become obdurate. Don't blame our problems on the enemy of Satan. Don't blame our problems on the person of the individual. It is us collectively; we must come out of individual silence and numbness to cooperatively address our systemic practices which is the culprit answerable to our problems. Insensible systemic practices abound around us. To list but a few, the grading system that does nothing but influences the students to focus their attention on grades. The promotion system that promotes nothing but a slavery system that benefits few. For instance, how many professors, students, and general citizens have genuinely benefited from the academic promotion system based on the number of the professor's journal publications? Disheartening few—the bulk of them never get ever read! Rather, students, professors, and citizens (in terms of their tax money), have been victimized by such a system, which has robbed life from the classroom, the office, the originally joyous pursuit of education. The list of insensible systemic practices can go on for quite a while.

Divorces may intuitively appear as individual problems. Yet when more than half of the population are divorced for at least one time, the causes of the problem are no longer individual. We must look at the way our organization designs our work, schedules our time, metes out reward and penalty. Is it because some organizational tyranny is robbing time and life of the father or mother out of their home? Is it because a full-time job or even double full-time jobs can no longer give a mere livelihood (What else can be a bigger insult to human intelligence and industry)?

As long as insensible systemic practices still exist, no laws, rules, grades, task quotas, accountability through statistical evidence, or any other type of reward and penalty practice can help remedy our deep-rooted and ubiquitous social problems and uneconomical waste. One day when systemic practices are based on simple and sensible principles, we'll no longer need those clumsy devices. Both the individual and organization will lead their lives by following the principles. When what we do makes sense, leadership and organization becomes straightforward. Life becomes simpler and economy becomes stronger. If half of human intelligence and industry are tapped, we will realize that we don't need to work for 40 hours a week to easily make a living. The simple life is one of joy, harmony, and fulfillment, both for the individual and for the organization. Motivation of human action should never be our clumsy system of reward and penalty (as reflected in grades, numbers, quotas, deadlines…). The only lasting and effective motivator of human actions is but joy with a sense of purpose.

4

Success and Failure

Mental lingering with negative feeling about a failed attempt will not help much; it will, however, likely detract the worrier from achievement of success with more endeavors coming up. On the one hand, it is completely understandable that we are constantly obsessed with worrying about success and failure. On the other hand, this worry can restrain us like an invisible yoke. Frequently, it is the detachment from this worry that enables athletes and artists to perform wonderfully. I often find my worry about failure rather debilitating, preventing me from savoring the moment, or from more efforts and trials. Worry about success and failure, though understandable and human, may make us all age more quickly. The most glowing successes I see are driven by a purpose, a passion, a love, a desire to see a certain beauty, to prove a certain method, or to savor the energy nurtured by continuous better performance. Frequently in reality, things turn out better than how we feel at the moment. We need to learn to free ourselves from the enslaving worry about failure.

Experience has taught me to be very wary about my love for success, especially when this success is defined on a basis of comparison. That is, when you judge whether you are successful by comparing yourself with others. There are a myriad of dangers in love for success thus defined. People espousing such success tend to be haughty before others not as "successful." On the other hand, they tend to be diffident and become even sycophants before others who are more "successful." We all know that hauteur/arrogance or diffidence will not serve us well in any performances and situations.

Occasionally I heard a voice considering me as a success. I feel grateful for that voice, yet I only consider myself a success when I can keep promises I make to myself, many of which I broke. It seems to me that the only energizing and humble success is when you can see a better self each every day; when you see that every day, you grow abler to achieve meaningful aims you define for yourself. These aims are formed not because they are a fashion, not because they will publicize your name, not because others' jealousy toward you makes you feel good, but because you believe in the inherent value and purpose of these aims, because you see a sustained wellspring of life in your efforts to realize these aims, because they give an energizing self in you along the days of your existence. I always believe that success, improperly defined, is a rather dangerous matter plaguing many of us. Success, properly defined, gives constant energy and joy, which really should be the fruit of true success. What makes it worse, countless organizations define their members' success improperly and evaluate these members inhumanely.

Every time when I drive and pass by a cemetery, I cannot help but reflect upon the meaning of life because, one day, we all will end up lying beneath one of the tombstones. When I remind myself that death is the ultimate terminal of this worldly life, I find it easier to persuade myself to concentrate on what is the more real in life, to guard against meaningless and enslaving feelings we impose on ourselves and on each other, simply because of a certain way we define success and evaluate ourselves.

I simply realize that I need to do things that make real sense to me and give me a solid sense of fulfillment. All in turn gives me a sense of confidence and self-capability. This sense is very important to me. I need it for every new day to feel that continued urge of life. This is also why I believe work is so important and inherent to a healthy life. One of my basic beliefs about human nature is that we are born with a love for work and creativity (Just look at my two little daughters: constantly energetic). However, in reality, we know that people hate work. This hatred against work, I believe, is not born, but cultivated, cultivated by society's definition of success and manner of evaluation, cultivated by how leaders and bosses lead their organizations and treat their employees. It is sad that work, which should be one of the most liberating experiences for life, more often than not turns out to be enslaving and debilitating to so many.

5

Childhood Dreaming

I often reminisce about my dreaming when a little kid. I was born into a poor family in a small rural village. The material life at that time was harsh. I used to cherish moments of solitude when I could quietly dream about having a better life for myself and my family. I would sit in the solitary field, looking into the infinite sky, and dream that one day I could have more money for books and better food. I would sit on the bank of the wide river, looking beyond the other bank, and speculate that people beyond the river and the mountains were living a life of abundance. I would sit by and visually follow the railroad until it merged into the horizon, and dream that, one day, I could take the train to go to Beijing and study in a college there. When I was a kid, I found it so much fun to look into all kinds of distances beyond the horizon and imagine about the wonderful possibilities of my life if I could live in those distant and new places. I'm glad that I still dream when I have moments of solitude (such as when it rains, snows, or when I'm stranded in some place by inclement weather), dreaming about how we as fellow beings can have more power and joy with each other instead of how we can have more power and joy over each other. Dreaming is a fun game to play, an exercise of imagination for the mind that my little daughters do all the time ("Daddy, when I grow up, can I do this?" "Daddy, if I do this, will I be able to…?"). We adults should not forget about dreaming and should practice it more often.

6

On Pursuit of Joy in Life

I so frequently think so hard about the question: what do I really want to get out of my life? Does life necessarily necessitate constant pain and stress?

I think so hard about the questions that I feel the acute pain of confusion. Yet deep inside me I know these questions are the simplest ones in the world. Every individual wants joy. Then why do so many of us have to experience almost constant pain and stress? The answer is also clear: We are not doing the necessary things, which are usually the simplest things. The bulk of our business is but busyness: the prodigious folly of doing our best for things that do not need to be done. I can't figure out any other thing so wasteful as doing with great efficiency that which doesn't have to be done at all.

The first problem is that we don't pursue the right things for our joy. We use totally wrong yardsticks to evaluate each other. Our evaluation and promotion systems no longer care whether what we do creates joy for ourselves and each other. Our evaluation of each other has been totally controlled by blind products from competition. Insensible quota systems are ubiquitous. The purpose, inherent value, and actual result of our work behind those quotas are left in tragic oblivion. The folly of a rat race is that even if I win it, I still remain a rat.

When life is pursued against the measurement of senseless quota systems, it can only be one of pain. The essence of life is a stable, eternal matter, and should by no means derive from a comparison with others. Evaluation systems that base work on comparison and stratification only destroy the essence of life and thus the joy of life, causing unnecessary pain, problems, and complications. One complication, for instance, is the created need for inspection and control, which has wasted enormous amounts of resources. Our current quota-and competition-based evaluations have totally denatured the essence of life, which can hardly ever be an internal matter. The innate matter of life has become extraneous: You have to depend on others to find whether you can be joyful; so much depends on a comparison and on how others are doing. The tragic inability of ours to control our individual destiny and concomitantly our communal destiny are almost guaranteed. Modern slavery may be less blatant than the historical one, but by no means less acute in causing pain. The feeling by countless of the debilitating ennui and the ubiquitous disease of procrastination are but two among the many conditions symptomatic of our modern slavery.

7

Is This a Free Society?

Freedom means having the time to engage in our heart-felt activities. But we feel more and more that we can't do this. Our society is making our values more and more singular and simplistic. These values can be easily summarized in two or three words: money, fame, and power. These things have long become goals in themselves so that countless people no longer care about how they get them or for what they have them. Numerous morbid conditions have emerged to plague us all. Just turn on the TV and see the range of morbid human engagements: people putting metal hooks into their backs and hoisted by helicopters; people eating human excrement in order to be known or get some money…We persuade each other that pain is the definition of joy. No wonder so many try so much on so varied things, not to live a life, but to escape pain existent in life: drinking, drugs, frivolous actions that make no sense, and most tragically, to consciously engage in pain upon themselves and others to get inured to pain. Pain is a ubiquitous condition. The more conscious the mind, the more sensitive the heart, the more acute is the pain. Suicide has historically been the terminus of many great minds and hearts—not their desired experiment, but their endeavor to escape from human pain. Students, as one group of us, consider their college years as "life in the tunnel," and hence the phrase "the end of tunnel" to signify gradation. Spontaneous savory of joy has long been replaced by envy, humiliation, hatred, and mistrust in so many interactions among us. Ironically, to achieve joy in this world frequently means the necessity to callus the heart and dull the mind. A questioning mind hardly can give a joyful heart. The slogan, "Don't make sense out of it; make numbers out of it," would perfectly apply to the modern condition of humanity.

How many times have you heard an internal weakening yet persistent voice calling out to your heart, "How much sense does all this make that I do in my waking hours?" Then how many times have you heard your mind plead your heart, "Stop telling me that; I'm already confused enough?" We are under an invisible and tyrannical power. The equation in this power is rather simple. Either victimize and be the winner or be victimized and be the loser. The game is played through a numerical accumulation. The winners in this game are few and losers are many. If "ten" has become the "mode," better make yourself a "fifteen." If "fifteen" has become the mode, better make yourself a "twenty." Our intelligence still hasn't dawned on us that a game with numbers is doomed to failure, for everyone. Not only that, a game with numbers create confusion, departmentalization, stress, unnecessary maintenance work, wasteful economics and the weakening of the lung because of short of breath. Compliance with the tyranny of numerical game has produced strife everywhere, within the family, in the office, and even in the bar. Again the game is one of either victimizing or being victimized. The fight and race does not stop until you either become totally senseless or retreat from the entire war. The moments of complete withdrawal from the war, though dishearteningly rare, are precious. They are moments when we find countless wonders from within and without. To be frank, sometimes I'm really damned tired of this senseless game of numerical accumulation that creates benefit for none but pain for many.

A few of our actions to ponder:

—To acquire power and fame by defeating other schools, educational institutions create rules and schedules which only crush the soul for learning.

—To get the end-of-month bonus, the police officer harasses innocent people so that they could fulfill the quota of catching a certain number of violators of traffic rules.

—To get a certain number of pages, students no longer care what how they write, but how much they write.

—To acquire a living and a name among a coterie, professors no longer care about how they could improve human conditions, but how they can impress the editors. The numerical game of publications has forced everyone to produce printed words, though rife with banal insignificances, that the reviewers find irrefutable. Unfortunately for social sciences, journal editors and reviewers focus their attention on the "irrefutability of arguments" and "comprehensives of literature reviews" which inevitably produce nothing but the most regurgitated papier-mâché of axiomatic banalities.

One day, when we get up in the morning to work, not for any fad, but for the welfare for ourselves and our fellows, we'll begin to find the liberating power of work. We'll begin to find meaning, joy, and life in the workplace. We'll begin to find that work and life do not have to be dichotomized as enemies. We will find more than enough time to help our students to learn and grow rather than mindlessly go through another semester of professorial routines. We will find that scholarship is a business of joy and camaraderie rather than the daily worry about tenure and promotion, which are currently done not to benefit, but to facilitate control and for some to have a name in the senseless game of numbers. One day, when work is longer defined according to numerical competition, but according to its benefit and significance, we will be able to give less time to making a living, and having more time to living a life. Our promises for freedom and pursuit of happiness will ever be closer to their fruition.

8

Is It Busyness or Business?

This paper addresses a seemingly ironic oxymoron: the baffling coexistence between the ubiquity of technology and the ubiquity of busyness in present human life.

Academics argue vehemently about technology and the present condition of our life. Obviously not everyone is in favor of technological advances. One argument against technology is that technology, opposite to its original purpose for efficiency, is actually making life busier. For instance, the invention of the washing machine is to make the drudgery of washing less time-consuming so that we have more time for leisure. The invention of the microwave oven is to make cooking more efficient.

Yet, ironically, despite the presence of technology, life for most people is still busy, actually so busy that they see life more as a matter of survival than as one of joy. Technology seems to have failed to fulfill its promise of efficiency and more leisure. Simple logic informs that efficiency and "busyness" are in contradiction.

But is it technology that makes life busy? Before blaming technology, I invite careful reflection upon the real causes of the "busyness" of life? Why is a student busy? Perhaps too much homework such as reading, writing, and tests. Why is a professor busy? Perhaps too many requirements for tenure and promotion. Why are the bosses busy? They have to do many things to keep an eye on their employees and to make sure "things go right." Generally speaking, most people are busy largely because they have to maintain a full-time job just to be able to make a living. The busier we are, the more we seem to thirst for technology in the hope that technology can give us super-human power. The solution of technology apparently is not working. How can it work? The problem is not technology. The problem is the evaluation system that happens in our workplace.

I believe that a serious confusion between performance and purpose is the culprit. Evaluation everywhere for the purpose of reward and promotion is based on the assumption that as long as you perform, you serve; as long as you do, you contribute; as long as you are busy, you produce. Then some obvious problems baffle the mind. Most professors publish articles that are rarely read. Whom are they serving? And yet no professor can lightly afford not to publish. Most students attend classes largely for acquisition of credits. They are not mentally involved because they know they will quickly forget, after the semester, what the professor's voice has been "covering." Whom is this education serving? And no student can lightly afford not to attend classes and not to do assignments. Similar conditions can largely apply to the majority of people who are doing some type of "job."

What is wrong here? It is not technology, but what Postman (1986, p.51) terms as technology-mindedness. This mentality focuses more on performance, speed, right procedures, details and, most importantly, quantity and numbers, rather than effectiveness, rightness, or the fulfillment of a clear and genuine purpose. It is not much exaggeration to say that numbers and statistics have become the singularly accepted evidence of progress almost everywhere in the "civilized" world: number of credits fulfilled, number of publications produced, number of meetings held and attended, number of panels accepted, number of products sold, number of dollars reaped, number of graduates degreed...Humans, the putatively most intelligent beings on this planet, still seem unable to distinguish between easy evidence and earnest evidence. This human folly has turned the workplace into a huge prison of mutual and self-oppression (Deming, 2000).

On the matters of evidence, millions of us are downright liars in the highest degree. Individual consciousness, emotions, popular common temperaments, the most basic common sense, none of these can any longer count as evidence. The blind espousal of numbers seems to have become the singularly acceptable and thus unchangeable norm of life. Yet we know, in the purity of our private consciousness, that this espousal may represent the biggest story of "the Emperor's New Clothes" up to now in human history. This lie that we collectively construct represents the worst economics any effort can conjure. It is costly in all terms. It is robbing the prime years of talented minds. It is wasting time that may be adequate to produce enough wealth to solve the problem of poverty. It is robbing millions of people of their life, although it may help provide these people with a living. Economics with the current evaluation philosophy and system, at best, represents sub-optimization rather than optimization (Deming, 2000). The farce of numbers can really be carried to the extreme. Just for one instance, each police officer this month has to "catch" at least 30 violators of traffic laws. Otherwise, please stand ready to lose your bonus for the month. Can we blame these officers for harassing innocent people?

There is no excuse to continue the current folly of the numerical evaluation system. It may be easy and expedient for the purpose of administration and bureacracy, or for the purpose of controlling people, but it is not in accordance with effective leadership and optimized economics. It continues simply because we do not yet know how to manage people, much less how to lead people. Yet ignorance can hardly serve as an excuse. If you do not know how to do the right thing, at least you can do nothing, which is even better than doing the wrong thing. I suspect that there may exist an unhealthy psychology. This psychology only accounts for the boss, but not for the public. This psychology relishes the false sense of security when seeing everyone busy. This psychology loves control over people and hates freedom to people. Who says we have abolished slavery in the civilized world!

References:

Deming, W.E. (2000). *The new economics: For industry, government, education.* Cambridge, MA: MIT Press.

Postman, N. (1986). *Amusing ourselves to death.* New York: Viking Press.

9

A New Humanism against the Societal Panopticon

In this essay, I will use the theory of Panopticon, introduced by Robins and Webster (1988), to analyze how technology, especially information technology, has invaded deeply into individuals' privacy and everyday life and has colonized it. I will advocate humanism as a possible solution to this problem.

However advanced a society is, however civilized a culture may be, it all has to be lived through the life of the individual. The quality of the individual's everyday life is the final yardstick for the progress in a society. In this light, we need a new humanism against a modern despot—the Panopticon built on informational and technological system.

The idea of "Panopticon" was first introduced by Jeremy Bentham and later elaborated by Michel Foucault. At the end of the 18th century, Jeremy Bentham outlined his plans for an institutional architecture of control. What Bentham devised was a general mechanism—applicable to prisons, asylums, schools, factories—for the automatic and uninterrupted functioning of institutional power and control. This mechanism, the Panopticon, is a building of circular structure with a series of individual cells built around a central "well"; at the center is an inspection tower from which each of the cells could be observed and monitored. A calculated illumination of the cells, along with the darkening and masking of the central tower, endows the "inspective force" with "the unbounded faculty of seeing without being seen" (Robins & Webster, 1988, p. 60). The concept now basically means that whatever the individual citizen does, it is under an omnipresent big eye. This systemic surveillance poses constant pressure upon the individual to conform and comply with the system. Thus, a dichotomy can easily occur between progress as defined by the system on the one hand, and progress defined by the individual on the other hand.

Let's first talk about how this Panopticon is formed in our society and how it functions in our life. We can trace the origin of Panopticon, first, to the industrial revolution, and then specifically to Taylorism. The former initiated the idea of standardized mass productions; the latter, the idea of standardized utilization of human workforce. The industrial revolution enabled us to see the great power of efficiency through the standardization of the production process. Taylor, excited by this power as many were (or still are), believed that great efficiency could also be brought out of the workforce if we ripped the worker of her[1] individuality by fitting her as a component cog unto the big machine of "scientific management." Gradually, efficiency became incorporated into and espoused by our culture as the ultimate terminus for human progress. Accordingly people naturally become serving resources (called "human resources" in a futile effort to make it sound more humane).

Efficiency calls for maximum production with the least amount of resources, including human resources. One way the management tries to achieve this is to keep some people unemployed or keep the employees under constant threat of being fired or make promotion based on peer competition. All this applies to higher education which has become nothing more than another type of industry, focused on efficiency. The unemployed waiting outside the gate injects into the hearts of the employed almost a constant consciousness of competition and pressure. This is a wonderful way of surveillance. No whips, video-cameras, or perquisites need to be used. Consequently the feeling of life as a race for survival becomes ubiquitous. This feeling will not change much despite further development in the society. For example, we suppose the latest developments in computer technology will facilitate scholarly production. But in reality, the computer because of its efficiency has helped put scholars under an obligation to produce more. The focus on more production is so intense and competitive that not much time is even left for reading and thinking. Scholars are beginning to experience "informania" more than they experience genuine scholarship (Heim, 1993). The ironic phenomenon has largely become the keyboard churning out words that people rarely (have time to) read. Yet every scholar is under invisible and powerful surveillance to produce more and more. Competition is putting no one's life at ease now.

The surveillance via competition does not seem to satisfy the appetite of the managerial or administrative mega-machine. New technologies are providing fur-

---

1.   To avoid technical inconvenience, I will use gender pronouns (he/she, her/his...) randomly in this essay.

ther means of surveillance or Panopticon. Computer technology has made it very easy to keep track of employees. One investigation shows that many companies begin to follow employees' emailing during work time to see whether they use their salaried time in an undesired way.

Panopticon, in its earlier stage, was achieved mechanically through the automated assembly line invented by Henry Ford. To work under such a line, the worker absolutely has to keep up with the automated pace. Failure to keep up with the pace will cause obvious systemic problems. No human inspection is needed. Humans have to obediently subject themselves to the machine-created pace.

On a larger scale, Panopticon is achieved through standardization and networking. Everything, if it can be claimed as modern or advanced, is standardized. The use of time is standardized through scheduled segmentation. Time is segmented and compartmentalized according to the different tasks of production, divided and subdivided to be used as productively and intensively as possible. The Panoptic power is articulated directly onto time, ensuring its control and guaranteeing its use. Not only the use of time in every single day is standardized, the use of time in one's whole life is also almost standardized. Since every profession has its standards and strict schedules, the trajectory of one's whole life in a specific profession generally becomes clearly predictable from even the very beginning. The employ has run pretty fast in order to complete the trajectory in a certain time. Competition has made life largely a game to race through the career trajectory as fast as possible. No inspection is needed. Most people will do it.

Consumerism, which has become a ruling norm of life, also plays a big role in standardizing the individual's everyday life. "Standardized packages" have replaced "almost everything people formerly did or made on their own" (Robins and Webster, 1988, p. 66). It will not be far in the future when we can see the whole nation using the same product to do the same thing at the same time of the day. Life some day may become of complete standardization with complete predictability. The end product of standardization is the philosophy of humans as "things of motion" rather than "persons of action."

> This process involves disciplinary efforts, both within the factory and across the fabric of everyday life: on the one hand, the division of labor, waged employment, time-shift, and the discipline of the "factory-prison"; on the other hand, the undermining of traditional culture (fairs, sports, etc.), the control f social space, and the moralization of the workforce through religion and schooling (Robins and Webster, 1988, p. 51).

As "things of motion," we largely function in a predetermined structural groove. Life necessary becomes a routine which in turn breeds boredom and ennui. The boredom from routine has made one wish prominent: "to complete what I have to do efficiently so that I can have some time for life." Well, most will never have "some time" for life, a fact inescapable from modern Panopticon. For some psychological peace, many begin to resort to numbness (e.g., via drinking and drugs or complete slavish resignation to whatever the daily schedule necessitates). Although numbness means a forfeiture of the right to the feeling of joy, it also means imperviousness to pain from routine, and a better promise of worldly efficiency and success. Efficiency and success as purpose of life has become the norm. Joy as purpose of life has become the anomaly. This is why it is not difficult to see why the order in the modern world is peace on the surface but war underneath.

More intangible and yet more powerful Panopticon is effected through singularized standards to basic human concepts such as success, happiness, and contribution. Since the society rewards the individual only according to its singularized standards, free choice by the individual has become extremely difficult. Free choices by the individual, even if non-harmful and conducive to public joy and well-being, can easily turn the individual into a social outcast or failure plagued with miserable poverty. Through singularized standards to basic human concepts, the Panoptic society tries to mobilize its citizens into a certain direction. But this mobilization can be very demobilizing and demoralizing because it often collides with another mobilization which grows out of the true wishes of the individual. The demobilizing power of societal mobilization is clearly and commonly seen in widespread apathy in the workforce and students.

The society as a whole comes to function as a giant Panoptic mechanism: automatic and continuous surveillance, along with centralized power and peripheral isolation, conspire to create a climate in which the inmates of society "not only *suspect*, but [are] assured, that whatever they do is known, even though that should not be the case" (Robins & Webster, 1988, p. 73).

After thousands of years' development in human civilization, we have overcome barbarianism like slavery, feudalism, and distorted communism, but we are now facing another barbarian force—societal Panopticon. This force can be more barbarian because its effects upon the individual are insidious and pervasive, enduring longer and deeper. Societal Panopticon breeds distrust everywhere. This growing distrust breeds problems. As long as mistrust grows, techniques, regulations, handbooks, laws won't help much in solving our problems.

The next question is how to change so as to restore real freedom and happiness to the individual? Unfortunately, Robins & Webster in their article did not provide much answer except saying that we should confront reality. Yes, we should. But how? I see the answer in a new humanism. In terms of technology, it means technology *for the people*, if technology cannot be of the people or by the people. This new humanism is the understanding and belief that progress is seen not in the development of the society as an abstract group, but in how the individual lives her own life through the mediation of the group; that life is achieved not through linear, titular progression (e.g., bachelor→master→Ph. D. or assistant professor→associate professor→full professor), but through multifaceted daily spontaneity; that every individual is good in nature, born with a wish to learn, to work, and to contribute; that the individual, once engaging her life as a daily multifaceted spontaneity, will be mobilized enough to produce more than adequate to satisfy not only her finite material needs, but also the more important need for life of joy; that real efficiency is better achieved through the intrinsic motivation coming out of the individual, than through structured organization of the individuals as mere component cogs of the societal mega-machine, which in reality wastes vast amounts of creative and productive human energy; that our material needs, which are naturally finite, have been exaggerated or distorted by the panoptically competitive race (e.g., the joy and art of cuisine has become very much trivialized and perfunctory for the sake of business efficiency); that the quality of life is seen not in the end product the individual achieves before death, but in every minute of the individual's everyday life…. Pardon me for engaging in the long list which may go on. In one word, this new humanism is a re-emphasis on the individual as "a person of action," and de-emphasis on or a fight against the structural organization of individuals as "things of motion." This new humanism "sees the essence of civilization not in a multiplication of wants but in the purification of human character" (Schumacher, 1997, p. 199).

The next question is how to achieve this humanism? Heidegger suggested Art, but we are not clear about how to actualize Art so that it becomes a balancing force against societal Panopticon. In history, some humanism was achieved through group movement, like slavery-abolition movement and civil rights movement. Some "weird" cultural phenomena also appeared in history as a resistance and fight against standardization and Panopticon. These may include the hippie movement. This kind of movement greatly decreases its power by making itself weird, which distances it from public sympathy.

What shall we do now? I do not approve of engaging in weirdness (e.g., extreme body piercing) because the wishes we are born with are for the natural and beautiful. Why should we use another form of weirdness (which can cause pain) or a distortion of our nature, to fight against the weirdness of societal Panopticon, when what we are trying to achieve is the natural humanism. I am thinking about several ways. I believe the fight against societal Panopticon can be carried out on three levels, the individual level, the community level, and the societal level.

Many individuals fight against all forms of societal tyranny by passive retreating. They indulge in a lethargic self-contentment. By doing this they turn themselves not only into social outcasts, but into failures of humanism itself. These people can never hope to pose themselves as an example of victory, or as a representative of the real humanist spirit. By their failure, they repel those with an incipient wish for humanism back into the clenching arms of the societal despot of Panopticon. Humanism should be a full-steam celebration of those natural human wishes for life, happiness, creativity and production. In this sense, a real humanist or a fighter for humanism, can be a complete failure according to conventional standards, but he should always remain victorious as a person, fresh as a spring flower. Inside the heart of the humanist is a genuine disdain against the societal Panoptic force, which is not for the betterment of the individual life, but for continuous efficient running of the Panoptic mega-machine—always at vast human costs.

The power of humanism increases if it is carried out on the community level. In a humanist community, a disdain against the societal Panopticon is shared by the community members. A conscious collective effort is maintained against societal Panopticon for a fuller fulfillment of the individual's potentiality. What is valued is not how well the individual conforms to insensible evaluations, but how well he enriches the minutes of his own life through sincere and significant work and contribution to the group. Reward is based not on a comparison/competition among community members, but on how better the individual does today than yesterday in following, conforming to and actualizing his own human spirit. In a human community, "people should be able to shape the basic social circumstances of their lives" (Sclove, 1997, p. 225). This belief has been empirically proved successful at least to some extent in the design of neighborhoods in Zurich, Switzerland, and in the Trudeslund co-housing community in Denmark started in the mid-1960s (Sclove, 1997, pp. 227–228). In these places, a person is judged by what he is, not by what he has. There are always several paragons of "the Right Livelihood" (Schumacher, 1997, p. 204) in the village for everybody to respect, to be inspired by, and to emulate. The community always gives precedence to individual happiness and sincere contribution to the community. The individual is always willing to work more as genuine acknowledgment of her sense of community. A social covenant is achieved not through compulsive Panoptic competition, but through empathic understanding.

Humanism can never be achieved with natural ease if it has not been realized on a societal level. We know the feeling of having the deafening, tyrannical societal voice shout into our ears every day. To achieve humanism on a societal level, scholars, especially those of social sciences and humanities, should unite their voices against our most inveterate and ubiquitous problems (Unfortunately, our system has completely conditioned our scholars to focus totally on promotion via publications, for which what matters is easy provability, leading to nothing in scholarship but coherent nonsense). Real humanist progress is seen more in mutual betterment than in individualistic accomplishments. The current scholarship, striking at the surface of minute phenomena for novelty and easy publishabiltiy, will not only lead us nowhere, but will breed a senseless and reckless approach to the important cause of education and science. Nothing is more tragic and wasteful than seeing thousands of scholars, people with talents, engage themselves in pettifogging on the leaves of evil, while the root of the tree of human spirit is rotting. I simply can not imagine how beautiful life will be if a Big Cooperation occurs among all our scholars, not to make his individual case, not to belabor the obvious again, not to produce "scholarship" which is little more than petty discoveries wrapped in the super-thick recycled paper of arcane language, but to humanize the societal mega-machine so that the productive and creative human spirit emerges and finds enough space in which to survive and bloom.

If the struggle between scientistic Panopticon and humanist empathy has stopped in the heart, it is high time to think and take actions about how to replace the pain-breeding Panoptic competition with the joy-nurturing humanist empathy.

References:

Deetz, S. (1990). Representation of interests and the new communication technologies: Issues in democracy and policy. In M. J. Medhurst, A. Gonzalez & T. R. Peterson (Eds.), <u>Communication and the culture of technology</u> (pp. 43-62). Pullman, WA: Washington State University Press.

Heim, M. (1993). Informania. In M. Heim, <u>The metaphysics of virtual reality</u> (pp. 3-11). New York: Oxford University Press.

Robins, K. & Webster, F. (1988). Cybernetic capitalism: Information, technology, everyday life. In V. Mosko & J. Wasko (Eds.), <u>The political economy of information</u> (pp. 45-75). Madison, WI: The University of Wisconsin Press.

Schumacher, E. F. (1997). Buddhist economics. In A. H. Teich (Ed.), <u>Technology and the future</u> (pp. 197-205). New York: St. Martin's Press.

Sclove, R. (1997). Technological politics as if democracy really mattered. In A. H. Teich (Ed.), <u>Technology and the future</u> (pp. 223-245). New York: St. Martin's Press.

Weedon, C. (1987). <u>Feminist practice and poststructuralist theory</u>. Oxford: Basil Blackwell.

10

Manifesto of the Individual of the New Millennium

The new millennium will come in just several hundred days. Since the birth of Christ, we have experienced two thousand years of time. Two thousand years is a long time during which so many dreams of ours have come true. Two thousand years is a short time during which our most important dreams, our deepest dreams, our most enduring dreams have not yet come true.

No other time is more proper than now, upon our entering the new millennium, for us to refresh those most important dreams, those deepest dreams, and those most enduring dreams of ours. We know those dear dreams have been dusted, dulled, or even destroyed despite all our struggles, prays, tears, and blood during the past two thousand years. The coming of this new millennium calls upon every and each one of us to declare those dear dreams with an unprecedented voice and hope, to refine those dreams with more lucid wisdom, and to design the realization of those dreams with ever greater passion.

So, let's declare our dream, clearer than ever before, and louder than every before: The new millennium is *a new age of the free individual.* We've long been fed up with all the forces that not only inflict pain in our body but also suffocate the spirit in our heart. These forces range from those crude ones to the most subtle and yet insidious ones. On the side of the crude forces, we suffer from war, dictatorship, and prejudice…On the side of subtle yet insidious forces, we suffer from bureaucracy, dogmatism, and insensible evaluation systems…All these forces try to kill the innately wonderful individual in every one of us because they know true freedom leads to the end of the corrupt power and tyranny of all forms.

In the new millennium, every individual, in the free pursuit of the noble work that reflects his dream, has the freedom to engage his hands and hearts in the noble way that he trusts. In the new millennium, every individual, depending on his honest heart and industrious hands, has her birthright to joy and happiness. In the new millennium, we no longer work day and night to supervise and control each other; we work with and for each other. In our new millennium, our governments, corporations, and communities no longer are despotic structures that supervise, control, restrain, and drive us. Our governments, corporations, and communities become the extended shadows of our dreams, our representative servants that facilitate the realization of the wonderful individual in every one of us.

My dear fellows, there is no other time more proper than now to declare our most dear dreams. Let our voices unite and declare, clearer than ever before and louder than ever before: Welcome the new millennium—our new age of the free individual, our new age of order, consistency, and, above all, simplicity.

11

Let our "God" Watch over our "Dog": Heidegger on Pessimism and Optimism about Technology

Heidegger offers an incisive understanding of pessimism about technology. This understanding helps to uplift us out of pessimism and enlightens about why optimism about technology is solidly within human reach. A superficial reading of Heidegger may only indicate his pessimism about technology, yet a more careful reading will reveal the ultimate belief of optimism by Heidegger about the relationship between human condition and technological advancements. This brief work first deconstructs pessimism about technology from a Heidegger perspective. Explanation will then be offered as to why optimism about technology and human condition is within our reach.

The bulk of Heidegger's (1977) "the Question Concerning Technology" appears arcane and gloomy. The concluding part, however, is inspiring, optimistic, and even poetic. This may be just natural. The road to victory oftentimes insinuates itself through the darkest and thickest night before it leads to the dawn—the true and the beautiful. This work of Heidegger represents an arduous effort to understand the essence of technology. This understanding promises the dawn of optimism seen through the dark night of pessimism about the self-propelling will of modern technology.

What is technology? It is both "a means to an end and a human activity" (Heidegger, 1977, p. 288). When we ignore the part that technology is a human activity, it becomes hard to understand why and how technology, the mere means to a human end, has now become almost the synonym to human progress and frequently lords over us as the surrogate to ultimate human purpose.

The essence of Technology is nothing technological. It is "enframing," the "gathering together of that setting-upon that sets upon man, i.e., challenges him forth, to reveal the real, in the mode of ordering, as standing-reserve" (Heidegger,

1977, p. 302). Technology starts with humankind "setting upon" nature to "bring forth" or "reveal" the real so that nature stands by as ready "reserves" for human use. The number and level of human actions of "setting-upon" nature gradually increase. Each action may produce a specific tool, technique, or technology. The discrete technique or technology does not seem to pose a danger. Yet when various technologies gather together, they form a self-regulating and self-propelling system with a will of their own. This system, because of its own will stemming from requirements of natural laws, then "sets upon" humankind and challenges it forth, not in a human-determined direction, but in a technologically necessitated direction. Here comes the danger of technology, claimed Heidegger.

Technology, according to Heidegger (1977), is an action of revealing or bringing forth into "appearance and concrete imagery" that in nature which can potentially serve humankind as "standing reserve." This is perhaps what is termed as "concretization" by Dumouchel (1995). I believe that the levels of "revealing" or "bringing forth" are different historically. Earlier, the level was lower. For instance, the craftsman set upon a stone and brought it into the shape of an ax. It could be claimed that the ax was simple enough to be easily subjected under the individual will of the craftsman; and that the ax directly represented the craftsman's effort to fulfill some specific wish of his. Later on, however, the action of "bringing forth" became much more complicated and interlocked. The interlocking complications led to the formation of a technological *system*, which began to acquire a self-regulating and a self-propelling independence (e.g., automation) from human will. It began to represent efforts not to fulfill primal, but secondary human wishes, which are determined not by human predilections, but are necessitated by technological advancements. Technological advancements require obedience on human part to obey sets of scientific laws and necessities. By this stage of technological development, human will finds itself easily subjected. Technology begins to "enframe" human will. This "enframing" produces the secondary wishes mentioned above. The concepts of efficiency and numerical evidence may be included under these secondary wishes, although efficiency can be at odds with effectiveness, and the genuine evidence may not be "numericalizable."

Under technological "enframing," humankind's primal wishes and secondary wishes can easily mingle. More blurred is the distinction between technological development and human progress. This is why a discrepancy is frequently felt between what humankind wants technology to do and what technology actually does. The humankind begins to see that technology not only serves them, but also imposes itself upon them, thrusting them down its technologically determined road and depriving them of freedom. Here is how technological determinism and the attendant pessimism come into being.

> "But where danger is, grows
> The saving power also…" (cited in Heidegger, 1977, p. 316)

The saving power lies exactly in the fact that we have become aware of the danger from technology. It is so, simply because our primal wishes still endure. As known to all, the feeling of pain is not necessarily bad. It also proves a well-functioning nerve system. "What endures primally out of the earliest beginning is what grants" (Heidegger, 1977, p. 313). If the primal wishes could grant power to technology for it to develop in its technological way, the primal wishes could also be able to grant power to the origin of these wishes (i.e., the humankind) to influence technology to develop in the human direction. A little lexical play may facilitate the comprehension. Technology could be considered, in final analysis, as *a* (not **the**) means to an end. I expediently call this means our "Dog" (letter capitalized, considering the present power of technology). Our primal wish(es) I call our "God." We should constantly plead our "God" to watch over our "Dog." This consciousness is what we should strive for with a systematic and sustained effort. The present problem seems to be not only that countless people among us begin to revere our "Dog" as our "God," but also that technology, in its long process of "revealing" or "unconcealing," has concealed from us a clear view of our "God." At such a time, Heideggar argues, we need another kind of technology (*technJ*). "Once there was a time when the bringing-forth of the true into the beautiful was called *technJ* "(Heidegger, 1977, p. 315). Heideggar admonishes that *technJ* should be embraced as the "new" technology so that the humankind yield "to the holding sway and the safekeeping of truth," so that "man [or woman] poetically dwells upon this earth" (Heidegger, 1977, p. 316).

Therefore, the question of technology is surely nothing technological; it is purely relational. Whether we have a problem with technology or not depends on how we maintain or negotiate or nurture the relationship between us and technology; how we negotiate or nurture our relationship between each other, which, to a large extent, is being mediated through technology. The problem with technology will be alleviated if we refuse, with a conscious will, to make technology the sole developmental direction for human life. In a time of democracy and modernity, we can argue against anybody, except, ironically, against technology. If we are told that it is the computer which is down, the case is closed (Postman, 1993). Technology has perhaps become one of the greatest autocratic factors in our time of democracy. Democracy should include the freedom to choose or not to choose technology, without any discrimination against the consequences from this choice. Freedom comes best when we surrender ourselves to but truth or primal wishes, which we should remain hopeful to achieve through the above-mentioned new *technJ*. Let all other factors, which may run out of our hands and pose a danger against us, be at the mercy of the truth; let our "God" watch over our "Dog"—so that we may hope to "dwell upon this earth poetically" (Heidegger, 1977, p. 316).

References:

Dumouchel, P. (1995). Gilbert Simondon's plea for a philosophy of technology. In A. Feenberg & A. Hannay (Eds.),

Technology and the politics of knowledge (pp. 255-271). Blooming, IN: Indiana Univeristy Press.

Heidegger, M. (1977). The question concerning technology. In D. F. Krell (Ed.), *Martin Heidegger: Basic writings* (pp. 287-317). New York: Haper & Row.

Postman, N. (1993). *Technopoly: The surrender of culture to technology.* New York: Vintage.

12

Some Reflections on Technology

The simpler form of technology was tools, and then techniques. The tools or techniques were invented and used to help satisfy existing human needs better. Originally, farmers used their implements to produce more food so that they did not have to starve. Washing machines help alleviate the drudgery housewives. In this line of thinking, with more technology, we should be able to have more and more leisure to engage in life, what we love (travel, reading, art…) instead of in just a livelihood (food, clothes, shelter, money, jobs…). But this is not the reality we are living. People talk more about survival for a livelihood than about savory of life. People are having no leisure and rushing with everything: traffic, food, work, family reunions…. People actually often think about how they can take more time from their leisure so that they can invest more time into their work for a better survival.

Then what is wrong with our technological inventions and gadgets if they are not giving us the leisure they are intended to achieve. To me technology itself is not the culprit. A knife is nothing bad. It becomes bad when used to scalp another fellow's head instead of to peel the potato. What matters with our technology is what kind of technology we are trying to invent and what we are using it for.

The intended purpose of technology is to satisfy our existent needs better. Yet technology not only does this, which is perfectly fine; technology also creates new needs for us. What is worse, technology seems to create new needs more quickly than it satisfies our old needs. Computer looks like a miraculous invention, which actually *is*. Yet is computer making our lives better or worse? Many find it hard to say. Now you have to spend at least fifteen minutes to get hold of some real human on the other side of the phone for solving your problem. When they tell you the computer is down, no further argument and reasoning would help.

It seems that we need to produce new technology in a controlled way, so that it better satisfies our real needs (our absolute needs for food, clothes, sex and shelter which constitute our innate need for joy) without creating more extraneous needs for us. More extraneous needs only mean more unloved work, which in turn means more pain. Our race with technology may easily become an accelerating one with more and more newly created needs. And we remain the loser in this race.

Technology must not acquire a life for itself and directs us. Technology must be invented and used always with a correct and controlling consciousness. Otherwise we will probably end up being enslaved instead of liberated by our own created technology. Anything (technology, laws, social conventions, culture, ideology), once created, tends to become reified objects and acquire a will of their own. It then poses a potential control over its creator if the invention is left alone with its own development. The only way to guard our fate when we create in order to serve, is by constantly keeping a conscious eye upon our creations. The next question becomes "What constitutes this conscious eye?"

13

Modern Scholarship Should be a Bridge between Scientism and Humanism

People would often find a gap between what they reflectively think and feel and what they unwittingly express. A similar form of possible distortion exists in the gap between personal identities and the images people live. One can look in a mirror and evaluate the body based on a host of external images while never carefully considering how the person feels or what is personally desired.... For example, an image may be constructed to enable one to succeed, yet at the moment of success the image rather than the person has the success, a success which means that the individual didn't get expressed at all (Deetz, 1990, p. 47).

When I read chapter seven in Van Patten (1996), "Future Trends and Issues in Higher Education," I see the trend and issue of humanism repeatedly discussed. In this essay, I will argue for the importance of humanism, and contend that modern scholars have the duty to maintain a balance between scientism and humanism.

There are two kinds of reason, the scientistic and the humanist. A gap between these two reasons, or precedence of one over the other, will not only cause the "gap" as described in the opening quotation, but also inflict us with problems of either postmodern heedlessness or traditionalist stagnation. In our age, scientism has apparently become almost the sole yardstick of rationality, making life to many people a drab matter of survival and adaptation to a flux of change and an impersonal system. It is high time that our scholars acted as a bridge between the two reasons, so that we live in the totality of our humanness, composed of both societal progress and individual happiness.

Scientism may be traced to industrialization. From mass production in industrialization, people realized the great producing power of efficiency which they could achieve from calculated mechanical organization of machines. Taylor was particularly inspired by the idea of efficiency. He believed that if compartmentalization and standardization could bring great efficiency out of machines, they should also be able to do so with humans. He immediately began to see running cogs in human hands, transmission rods in human limbs, and control buttons in human eyes. Taylor believed that a meticulously calculated synchronization of these "cogs, rods, and buttons," scientifically embedded into the automated mega-machines, would produce wonders. It all did. Work no longer was a cooperative effort, a way of life that assumed community and sharing. Instead, work became a routine of very restricted content, an absolute evil to put up with for the acquisition of enough means to escape work. The concept of human was changed. The "changed concept of man [and woman] is best described by the word 'scientistic,' a term which denotes the application of scientific assumptions to subjects which are not wholly comprised of naturalistic phenomena" (Weaver, 1963, p. 1045).

When efficiency became the over-ruling idea, it "came to be believed increasingly that to think validly was to think scientifically, and that subject matters made no difference" (Weaver, 1963, p. 1045). Logical validity has become the yardstick of scholarship. The scholar "would work upon one thing as indifferently as upon another. He [or she] would be an eviscerated creature or a dispassionate one, standing in the same relationship to the realities of the world as the thinking technique stands to the data on which it is employed. He would be a thinking robot, a concept which horrifies us precisely because the robot has nothing to think about" (Weaver, 1963, p. 1047). Many of our scholars can take any phenomenon in reality as the subject of her[1] study. After a logical processing of her collected data, she provides us with conclusions and discoveries. Scholars use cause-effect analysis method as their major method for investigation. Again according to Weaver, "cause and effect is a lower-order source of argument because it deals in the realm of the phenomenal (Weaver, 1963, p. 1050). Since phenomena in our reality have proliferated because of many new technologies, scholarly study has also proliferated. It tends to make the world pile up bodies of specialized knowledge which no one person can hope to command. To maintain objectivity in scholarship, many norms are stipulated in terms of language use.

---

1.   To avoid mechanical inconvenience, I will use gender pronouns (he/she, her/him...) randomly in this essay.

Yet language itself is a subjectively born, intimate, and value-laden vehicle. Also when the target is aimed at scholastic objectivity, what tends to be ignored is the fact that the scholar, when she does her research, is always selecting, emphasizing this and de-emphasizing that. Objectivity is probably not achieved to a substantial degree without the scholar's personal honesty and belief in his responsibility via his research toward his fellow people.

In light of scientism, rarely are human needs considered when financial resources are limited. Rarely are social, non-economic factors assessed in choosing where to place resources for development. Many university departments, though professionally prestigious, find it hard to survive mainly because of financial problems. Scientism believes that good organization brings about good employees. But it tends to forget that no organization is powerful enough to regulate the behaviors of its employees any more than a state could enforce its laws, without organized consent. Scientism has made efficiency "the primary criteria for the evaluation of all of life. The 'non-rational' aspects of life become inconveniences to be ordered and brought under control" (Deetz, 1990, p. 46). The attempt to accomplish practical ends through what Habermas (1984) called technical-instrumental reasoning has become a guiding mode of rationality superseding all other possible forms of reason. John Dewey noted in his *Individualism Old and New*, "quantification, mechanization and standardization are the marks of Americanization that is conquering the world" (cited in Van Patten, 1996, p. 80). The domination of scientism creates a two-sided problem: one regarding the formation of self-identity and the conception of self-interest and another regarding the social opportunity for the expression of self-identity and self-interest. Habermas (1984) calls this problem systematically distorted communication. Systems of thought, expression, and communication medium may contain embedded values that are at odds with the person's own values, if such a person could openly assess them. Scientism "interpellates individuals into subjects through complex, 'forgotten' inter-discourses whereby each subject has a signified, self-evident reality which is 'perceived-accepted-submitted to" (Deetz, 1990, p. 48). Consequently the individual becomes one-dimensional person, molded into the subject assigned to her by the society. Thus life becomes a routine of restricted content to many people. They live in "the restricted environment of reductionism" (Van Patten, 1996, p. 80). The life-world institutions that provide consensual understanding are overloaded by the need for ever more system coordination (Habermas, 1975).

Since the western concept of political democracy rests on a 'natural' right of the individual to have her interests fairly represented in matters that affect her well-being and pursuit of happiness, enough scholars must take some of their attention from societal progress to the individual person's life. For the individual, "[t]he meaning of experience is perhaps the most crucial struggle for meaning since it involves personal, psychic, and emotional investment on the part of the individual" (Weedon, 1987, p. 79). To improve reality which is seen through the eye of the individual, much scholarship should shift from scientism to humanism.

In contrast to scientism, humanism is the "soft" science which, in many eyes, does not help more efficient production at all. The majority of students, in choosing majors, tend to avoid things which are human: feelings, emotions, things difficult to logically define and analyze, including art, music, literature.... On the other hand, hard sciences, especially those which give a better promise to generate more hard cash, become more popular. Computer science and electronics engineering may be the leaders of these "hard" sciences. Famous computer softwares will acquire much more attention than famous speeches, because the former addresses logically tangible and specific problems, which are good subject matter for scholarship. Human reason, on the other hand, is too soft to be scholarly.

The consequence of the rise of scientism and the decline of humanism is great numbers of unhappy individuals who function as component "running cogs" to keep the huge "civilization machine" running. Yet humans, in nature, tend to be more holistic and emotional than analytical and logical. "Just what comprises humanism is not a simple matter for analysis. Rationality is an indispensable part to be sure, yet humanity includes emotionality, or the capacity to feel and suffer, to know pleasure, and it includes the capacity for aesthetic satisfaction, and, what can be only suggested, a yearning to be in relation with something infinite" (Weaver, 1963, p. 1045). When humanness is considered as "a drag on progress," and human qualities as weaknesses, many people have ignored the essence of being a human. These people may choose to ignore humanness within them, but it does not go away. Thus when they organize their lives according to scientism, humanism pops up buoyantly in conflict with scientism. This conflict between scientism and humanism, which translates into the most popular war between systemic requirements and private yet common believes, causes great apathy. Students hate homework. Employees hate office work. Many teachers do not love teaching.... In one word, countless people tend to avoid what they do as their *job*. Many universities have become homes "of lost causes, and forsaken beliefs, and unpopular names, and impossible loyalties" (Mathew Arnold). Students are asked to follow a valid reasoning without responding to reality. How can education hope to succeed by reasoning against reality? Most students are learning more and more, but they are living less and less. Human sensibility is surrendering to intelligence.

Scientism tells us that calculated organization is good for production. Therefore, modern life is organized as tightly as possible: college courses, schedules, work days and holidays, paper formats, entertainment, eating, sleeping.... Organization tries to make a "straight-cut ditch" of humanism, which is "a free, meandering brook" (Thoreau). "[T]things would be better if men did not give in so far to being human in the humanistic sense. In the shadow of the victories of science, his humanism fell into progressive disparagement" (Weaver, 1963, p. 1045). When humanism falls into progressive disparagement, this world becomes productive of much frustration. It is now the turn of our wisdom-endowed scholars to reverse this tendency.

A re-emphasis on humanism or human reason will help lead more toward a better human condition, which is lived after all by individual persons than by any abstract groups. The subject of human reason is the whole person, her nature as a pathetic being, that is, a being feeling and suffering. The human is not so much a logical entity as an emotional one. More scholars should take an effort to re-assure the more important position of humanity sciences in education and life. The "emotional" sciences address the person in his totality, thus in his humanness. "[O]rganizationl stewards need to be ever vigilant in supporting the humane use of human beings" (Van Patten, 1996, p. 79). Chancellor Emeritus William Pearson Tolley of Syracuse University wrote, "Education should deal with the whole [person]...Schools and colleges should minister as best they can to the needs of the whole [person]" (cited on Van Patten, 1996, p. 84). It is first the responsibility of scholars to help with this task. Personally, I frequently have to find inspiration for survival from famous speeches rather than from scholarly articles because these speeches talk to me by addressing me as what I am. They talk about what I really feel. They talk about the mundane, my everyday life. They take into account my dreams, hopes, fears, and present circumstances. In one word, they talk to the real person. As again Weaver says, "A speech intended to persuade achieves little unless it takes into account how men are reacting subjectively to their hopes and fears and their special circumstances" (Weaver, 1963, p. 1045). Humanities and social sciences are a kind of speech if what they are trying to do is to influence the students in a certain way.

Students and teachers are not creatures "abstracted from time and place." Their lives are very much molded by what happens in every minute and every location in their daily living. If science deals with the abstract and the universal, human reason is near the other end, dealing in significant part with the particular and the concrete. Human reason takes into account what science deliberately, to satisfy its own purposes, leaves out. That is, human reason "always comes to us in well-fleshed words, and that is because it must deal with the world, the thickness, stubbornness, and power of it" (Weaver, 1963, p. 1047). Emerson said, "Perhaps the time is already come when…the sluggard intellect of this continent will look from under its iron lids and fill the postponed expectation of the world with something better than the exertions of mechanical skill" (1837, p. 134). Emerson believed that "the near, the low, the common" should be "explored and poet-ized," that "the poor, the feelings of the child, the philosophy of the street, the meaning of household life" should be "the topics of the time." (1837, p. 136). Human reason embraces us not as resources for efficient production and targets for heedless consumption, but as the end for everything else. It tries to restore us the "right livelihood," a balanced life between materialist heedlessness and tradi-tionalist stagnation. Human reason tries to restore dignity into the person by reminding him that he is a self-conscious individual with a lively human spirit. Human reason, with its holistic and persistent voice, always tries to remind us where we truly want to go so that scientism, merely as the accelerator of the car of civilization, does not get us far off the proper track. In this age of reason, one of the most important responsibilities of scholars is to advocate and spread human-ism so that reason is protected from itself.

Humanism seen in the whole conspectus of its function is an art of emphasis embodying an order of desire. Only when scholars address the desire can they get to address the soul; only when they address the soul can they get to address the person. Scholars need to distinguish between the real desire from the soul and the false desire from the societal call. They must use humanism as an antidote against scientism so that the modern, organized, social life progresses in conformity with human essence. Thus can scholars hope to nurture the real civilization which is concretely lived through the life of the individual.

Humanism, in its highest form, tries to make people see the "unchanging essences" in their spirit. Once it succeeds in this, life of many people will no longer remain a struggle to keep their heads above the water of the flux of change; they will stay home with themselves. For civilization to progress in its true sense, a balance must be achieved between scientism and humanism. This is, first, the task of modern scholars, who represent the center of light and wisdom.

References:

Deetz, S. (1990). Representation of interests and the new communication technologies: Issues in democracy and policy. In M. J. Medhurst, A. Gonzalez & T. R. Peterson (Eds.), <u>Communication and the culture of technology</u> (pp. 43-62). Pullman, WA: Washington State University Press.

Emerson, R. W. (1837). The American scholar. In Y. S. Shi (Trans.), <u>One hundred famous speeches</u> (pp. 134-139). Beijing, China: China Foreign Translation Publishing Company.

Habermas. (1984). <u>The theory of communicative action, volume I: Reason and the rationalization of society</u>. trans. T. McCarthy. Boston: Beacon Press.

Van Patten, J. J. (1996). <u>The culture of higher education: A case study approach</u>. Lanham, Maryland: University Press of America.

Weedon, C. (1987). <u>Feminist practice and poststructuralist theory</u>. Oxford: Basil Blackwell.

Weaver, R. (1963). Language is sermonic. In P. Bizzel & B. Herzberg (Eds.). (1990), <u>The rhetorical tradition: Readings from classical times to the present</u> (pp. 1044-54). Boston: Bedford/St. Martin.

14

The Despotism of Group Values and the Condition of our Life

The farther away we are from conscious individual values, values that emerge in free solitude, the more likely we commit serious crimes, both against others and ourselves.

A desirable society should have the sincerity and practical mechanism to accommodate conscious individual values and concerns, so long as these values and concerns are not harmful to others. The problem now is that it takes great, great amount of courage to maintain individual interests and concerns. Though diversity is espoused, societal values nurtured and advocated by current reward systems are ubiquitous and inescapable and sadly have become yardsticks for success. A conventionally successful life is hardly one of joy. It's perplexing how a joyless life can be claimed as a successful one. Societal values strengthened by widespread human practices are the worst despots in our life; pursuit of these values offers nothing but confusion, fatigue, pessimism, busyness, and eventually pain. Even winners in the rat race of our defined life are not joyful; many of them still feel like "rats." The feeling of "busyness" has become fashionable reality and mentality. However, aversion to this feeling is perfectly mirrored in the ubiquitous disease of procrastination. The widespread practice of procrastination can by no means indicate the presence of joy.

Societal values buttressed by current reward systems are more vicious despots than those real ones in history. These values have become panoptic, an all-inclusive blanket no one can escape. The bulk of human actions are no longer products of conscious individual dreams, aspirations, and joys, but passive reflections of instituted human practices, the momentum of which is so strong that it carries everything it touches into its muddy stream. The despots of societal practices and values are omnipresent and omnipotent and yet intangible, making them to hard to fight with. We are bound to be an exile: either a social exile when you defy societal values or a psychological exile when you defy your heart. There is almost an unbridgeable chasm between societal values and practices and conscious individual dreams and aspirations.

Societal values have made deception an accepted fact of life, so much so that we have long been numb to this deception. Take for one instance, professors are forced not to teach but give their time to publications that help promotion. These publications, ironically, are hardly read by anyone. The whole cycle of actions here is simply confusing: Students and taxpayers pay the professors for education, our administrators and systematic practices force professors to churn out publications (where the worst case is one based on competition so that no one eventually wins—"five" is a loser to "ten" which in turn is a loser to "fifteen"). And no one ever-hardly reads these publications, the bulk of which are largely coherent nonsense and insignificances. Thus in final analysis, we all seem to throw our money away into a nameless and fathomless valley. This cycle of actions have made boredom and ennui the synonym of education. An interesting classroom has rather become anomalous. Because of its nature and purpose, education, if of any success, cannot but be the most interesting time in the student's life.

If we send but half an hour every day reflecting on the purpose of our education, government, and business, we'd surprisingly find so much of what we do are not only unnecessary but, which is even worse, wasteful and debilitating. No economics can be more wasteful than one where everyone does his or her best doing things that never need to be done.

PART IV

China

1

Prejudices and Discriminations in China

I grew up in a small rural village in central China. I well understand the harsh life of those migrant working women trying to earn a living in urban China. Although I can be so liberal in thinking as to be shocking to myself, I found prostitution (mostly forced) an absolutely a sin against women. It is a devastating damage to their body, mind, and soul. Human beings, allegedly the most advanced species on this planet, still often don't know how to pursue joy in a jointly pleasing manner. Ironic tragedies created by these advanced beings still plague all of us and disgrace the face of our residence of the earth. I consider joy via forced prostitution (either for men clientele or women clientele) as one of these ironic tragedies.

One other sad thing I frequently see in China is the prejudice that Chinese hold against each other: the rich against the poor, the powerful against the weak, and the urban against the rural. The prejudice that the urban population holds against the rural population stands out poignantly in my mind because it is almost omnipresent in China. Very often, the former would hardly make any effort even to hide that prejudice and contempt against the country people. I come from a rural village and I understand prejudice against people of lower social stations is actually prejudice and contempt against my own past when I was not fortunate as I am now. Another prejudice in my country is the contempt by governmental officials against the citizens. Chinese consulate and embassy officers working in the U.S. too often are not polite at all to their Chinese fellows visiting those offices. Countless governmental officials within China are not polite enough to the citizens either. My experience with some local officials in my hometown rankles in my mind because their lack of care and empathy was appalling and humiliating. American people would find this hard to understand. The mentality in the U.S. is that every citizen automatically expects and largely receives courteous and pleasant service from local, state, and federal officers because, they believe, they pay for the officers' salary with their tax money. Sadly, this is not the case in my country.

2

The Fifth Discipline in the Context of Chinese Organizations

China after the establishment of the People's Republic of China (PRC) in 1949 experienced two completely different economic eras, initiated respectively by our two great former leaders, Mao Zedong and Deng Xiaoping. Yet both of the eras have their own inherent problems. Growing up and having worked for almost 30 years in China, I have long become familiar with the problems. And I believe that the majority of the populace are still plagued with organizational problems in China.

After entering college in 1986, I have been thinking about the problems in Chinese organizations, trying to figure out their causes and solutions. My observations, reading and thinking gradually gave me the personal conclusion that no major solutions will come about without working out a harmonized holistic system. After my recent reading of Peter Senge's popular book *The Fifth Discipline: the Art and Practice of Learning Organization*, I am very glad to find much resonance and revelation in Senge's ideas, put in the context of Chinese organizations. In this paper, I wish to explain and analyze organizational problems in China through the lens of Senge's idea of the learning organization. My major attention will be given to the present period of China, because we cannot change Mao's period, which has become history.

According to Senge, what constitutes a learning organization are the following five factors: systems thinking, personal mastery, mental models, building shared vision, and team learning. These factors form an organic whole. This paper is structured in accordance with Senge's theory of the learning organization. The first two (systems thinking and personal mastery) of the five disciplines will be talked about separately. The last three (mental models, building shared vision, and team learning) will be grouped together because they contain a common theme.

1. Systems Thinking

Systems thinking is the central idea of Senge's five disciplines. Systems thinking signifies universal principles that govern every single and imaginable factor within a group, be the group as small as a family or as big as the world (Senge, 1990). The factors within the system interact and influence each other. If these factors are not in place with each other, problems occur. This can be illustrated with what has been happening within Chinese organizations.

(1) **In Chinese organizations, many rules, legal or otherwise, are not universally enforced.** Millions in China are cynical about rules, policies, and even laws. The most important reason is probably that rules don't carry force with people of power. The same crimes are punished drastically differently, depending on who the perpetrator is (Dorn and Wang, 1990). How do you educate the people to obey the law? The only way to succeed is if that law applies to everyone, including governmental officials and their families. As long as there is a privileged class that cannot be touched by law, one cannot expect the people to obey the law well. "Unless and until a political system rooted in law, rather than personal power, is firmly established in China, the road to the future will always be full of twists and turns" (Cheng, 1988, p. 543).

(2) **People have two value systems, one within their organizations and one without.** Values advocated within and outside of the Chinese organization are almost opposite. Organizational and governmental leadership advocate "contribution and sacrifice." The general society, however, espouses and practices self-interests and possession. This dichotomy in the value system breeds great confusion and cynicism within the person and among the people. Given the much bigger size and pervasiveness of the general society compared with that of an organization, and given that people generally believe their real lives are lived in the society instead of in their respective organizations, the majority in China tend to adopt social values rather than their organizational values. Thus people within the organization act with the social values, the opposite of the organizational values. The necessary result is employees' low morale and their cynicism towards the organizational mission and goals. According to Dorn and Wang (1990), in a TV factory in Shanghai, quality examiners sit down and turn on the TV sets in front them; not to check the quality but to watch their favorite programs.

(3) **The system of prices is not uniform.** It is simply not systemic to keep half of China's economy under state planning and half of it free. In the course of implementing Deng Xiaoping's policy, Zhao Ziyang and Hu Yaobang both realized that it was impossible to keep half of China's economy under state planning

and half of it free. For one thing, the state-owned enterprises got their raw materials from government agencies at very low subsidized prices, and side by side with that arrangement was a free market for the same materials at prices five to eight times as high. In such a configuration, the opportunity for corruption is tremendous. Anyone who had access to government-supplied raw materials could sell them on the free market for an easy profit. Some of the state-owned factories could even afford to pay their workers without producing anything at all. So much can be based on personal relations and power. Factory managers without connections were obliged to buy raw materials on the free market. Of course, the children and associates of powerful government officials were at a great advantage because they had connections. Tremendous corruption is ubiquitous, and the economy has been in a constant state of confusion (Cheng, 1988).

According to *China News Digest* (Oct. 16, 1997, website: http://www.cnd.org), a poll by the State Economic Structure Reform Committee of 42 state-owned enterprises in the provinces of Liaoning, Jilin and Heilongjiang showed that among 1250 employees and senior leaders in the enterprises, 1042 (83.3%) were dissatisfied with reform policies concerning state-owned enterprises. The majority of people believe that most leaders are involved in corruption. More than 60% of the leaders themselves admit in the poll that they are involved in some kind of bribery and other forms of corruption.

(4) The politically centralized system and the economically free market system may cause practical problems. Ending the widespread corrupt practices in Chinese organizations requires more than exhortations for good behavior on the part of state officials; it requires effective constitutional constraints on the state's economic powers. As long as most of the economic cards are held by the state, politics will continue to dominate economics. When prices are set in Beijing, they must be monitored and enforced; when prices are set by the market, the forces of demand and supply serve to automatically bring individual plans into consistency without a coercive state planning agency. In the open market, therefore, there is no need to bribe suppliers to ensure delivery; the prevailing market price provides the necessary information and incentive. If China does not adjust its political system to bring it in more resonance with its economic system, its economy will continue to be prone to corruption, waste, and bubbles of spuriousness.

Investment decisions in China are placed at the boundary between bureaucratic control and market forces, the theory being that enterprise managers would advance investment proposals in response to the market while government authorities retained the right of final approval in the light of broader-based priorities. It is in doubt that enterprises can pursue policies that are rational in terms of market forces if they have to remain subject to significant administrative influence. Chinese government pays nearly $11 billion in subsidies to support state-owned enterprises (Southerland, 1988).

(5) Systems thinking is not reflected in our goal setting. Systems thinking draws our attentions to the long distance between causes and effects. Short-term goals may give us immediate and great progress, but may also cause more serious future problems. In Chinese organizations, young leaders tend to put attention on short-term gains for purpose of good administrative evaluations and career promotion. What they care about is *today* when they are in power. They couldn't care less is *tomorrow* when they may be out of power. "Young leaders, lacking either revolutionary credentials or personal charisma, will be even more inclined to seek quick payoffs to attract the support of powerful bureaucratic actors, including provincial and military leaders" (Hamrin, 1990, p. 212). The compulsion for quick gain has infused the popular culture as well as the bureaucratic culture. Some have called China a 'nation of scavenger' that seeks immediate material gain before the opportunity passes and never to return. One Chinese sociologist has attributed this behavior to the mass uncertainty that stems from the fragility of a reform program based on short-term policy pronouncements rather than well-established law. The brain master of the Reform, Deng Xiaoping, once said, "We need to fumble for the stepping stones to ford the river." Lack of long-term principles is one symptom of non-systemic thinking. Knowing that leaders have changed and will change policies overnight, managers, workers, and merchants all use their newly given autonomy to exhaust state assets rather than to invest for the future. The contradiction between high expectations for achieving immediate prosperity and the constraints imposed by resource realities will grow and is likely to produce severe economic, social, and political strains.

(6) Systems thinking dictates that technocratic solutions will not work for socio-economic problems. In order to avoid attention being turned to the political system, Chinese leaders have the tendency to turn to technocratic solutions for socio-economic problems. This bent of mind ensures that democratic reforms lag behind both the public demand and the requirements from continued scientific progress. Deng's legacy of centrally initiated and controlled reformism, combined with the social engineering mentality and strong fears of social instability in the rising leadership generations that suffered from the Cultural Revolution, has fostered a decided lean toward policies of social and economic order by adopting technocratic solutions to socio-economic problems. Popular demands for political expression and desires for personal freedom weigh lightly (e.g. Hamrin,

1990). According to Leider (1996), leaders often shy away from the human side of the organizational problems because they are tougher to deal with. Leaders are more comfortable with the technical or financial tasks than with the human issues. They say, "I don't want to get into all that soft stuff. I just want to get results."

Party intellectuals during Hu Yaobang's period "believed that only radical system-wide reform, including a shakeup of the cadre system, could regain popular support for the regional regime and bring about a renewal of public morality" (Hamrin, 1990, p. 66).

We can feel a clear emphasis from our government upon technology instead of upon knowledge. The former produces easy-to-govern machine-like people. The latter produces intelligent people who can easily find that the root cause of many of our problems lies with our governmental system.

2. Personal Mastery

Personal mastery means: (a) a clear understanding of our personal mission and of the connection between this mission and the big mission of the community we live in; (b) an ability to have control over our own lives and lead our lives according to our own designs.

(1) Personal mastery suggests the ability on the part of the individual to see a connection between his/her personal concerns and the group concerns. Personal mastery also suggests an ability to transcend our own personal concerns so that our group concerns can be better fulfilled.

The lack of the above-mentioned abilities on the part of the individual was what caused the problems during our commune period. In the New China's first economic era, we had the commune system. The whole system was highly planned by the central government, which owned the production means. People worked for the commune's production team and were allotted their share of pay presumably according to their work. Yet people lacked the shared vision, on the larger level, that they were together building their own "big happy life." Only when people could see a more direct connection between their personal good and what they were doing as a group, they worked hard. Deng's Reform proved this point. The communal movement at its initial stage was quite successful. The process was gradual, cautious, and carried out on a small scale in the form of cooperative farms. "Although population increased 14.8 percent between 1952 and 1958, the gross value of agriculture measured in 1952 prices increased 278 percent, and grain output increased 21.9 percent in the same period" (Dorn and

Wang, 1990, p. 153). Yet "[t]he collective farm did not solve the problem of mobilizing labor for large projects, such as irrigation canals, dams, or the like. These kinds of projects would, in general, require the simultaneous participation of laborers from several dozen collective farms" (Dorn and Wang, 1990, p. 153). Gradually, the communes (composed of dozens of collective farms) resulted in the profound agricultural crisis that occurred between 1959 and 1961. The gross output of agriculture fell 14 percent in 1959, 12 percent in 1960, and another 2.5 percent in 1961. Most devastatingly, grain output plummeted by 15 percent in 1959, plunged another 16 percent in 1960, and remained at the same low level for another year. It is estimated that crop failures resulted in 30 million excess deaths in 1958-1961 (Dutt, 1967). The commune movement failed to enable the people to see a direct connection between their personal welfare and the success of the commune. When people are not ready by being personally transformed, big projects like our communes are doomed to failure.

Leaders, on the other hand, also should learn a lesson from the failure of our commune system. They must understand that the great majority of the public perceive the organization from their personal problems and goals. If the people can't see a connection, direct or indirect, between their personal problems and the organizational goals, they won't feel much voluntary motivation to carry out the organizational goal. Real leadership must be able to show clearly this connection, no matter how indirect this connection may appear. The next step for the leader is to help his/her people transcend their personal problems and concerns to fulfill the organizational goals better. All this is very important because, in this interconnected world, the fulfillment of the organizational goal frequently forms the foundation for that of personal goals.

(2) Personal mastery also suggests a sense of personal control over one's life, without which, the "mastery" part may be difficult to occur.

Personal control over one's life can be difficult to achieve in Chinese organizations. When production means (e.g., of state-owned enterprises) are in the hands of the state and all the important economic decisions are left to the state, individuals become subservient to the ruling elite and economic decisions become the subject of political influence. In such a political-economic order, incentives to produce necessarily suffer. This has been the experience in China. Take the case of Chinese agriculture for example. Even though China's agricultural reform enlarged the opportunities of farmers to use the land at their disposal, it did not extend full ownership rights. The communes were abolished and individual farming was allowed on a family basis. However, farmers were not allowed to own the land they farmed. They merely sign a contract with the government for a number of years. As such, they have little incentive to reinvest their money to improve their farms. Instead, they use the money for other purposes (Dorn and Wang, 1990).

Likewise, in the cities, for quite some time the reform allowed for small-scale industries, but those entrepreneurs who earned profits were not allowed to expand their businesses—because they were limited to small-scale firms to supplement the nationalized industries. Since entrepreneurs cannot own, develop, or invest their profits, they have no real incentive to innovate or be overly productive. According to Raffini (1993), the sense of control is an important component to motivation.

The major obstacle to continued personal mastery and liberalization, however, is the coupling of political and economic power. The politicians and bureaucrats who run China's state enterprises refuse to release their iron grip on the socioeconomic system. As long as these bureaucrats control the bulk of investment resources and dominate the interests of the newly emerging entrepreneurial class, private individuals will lack the freedom to decide where to invest their savings for the highest return and resources will be locked into unprofitable uses and even into corruption.

As to points three, four, and five of Senge's five disciplines, I'd like to talk about them as a group instead of one by one, because common ideas thread through these points. The following quotations serve as a brief summary of points three, four, and five of the five disciplines:

3. Mental Models

"Mental models are deeply ingrained assumptions, generalizations, or even pictures or images that influence how we understand the world and how we take action.

The discipline of working with mental models starts with turning the mirror inward; learning to unearth our internal pictures of the world, to bring them to the surface and hold them rigorously to scrutiny. It also includes the ability to carry on "learningful" conversations that balance inquiry and advocacy, where people expose their own thinking effectively and make that thinking open to the influence of others" (Senge, 1990, p. 8).

4. Building Shared Vision

"The practice of shared vision involves the skills of "unearthing shared 'pictures of the future' that foster genuine commitment and enrollment rather than compliance. In mastering this discipline, leaders learn the counterproductiveness of trying to dictate a vision, no matter how heartfelt" (Senge, 1990, p. 9).

5. Team Learning

"The discipline of team learning starts with 'dialogue,' the capacity of members of a team to suspend assumptions and enter into a genuine 'thinking together.'

The discipline of dialogue also involves learning how to recognize the patterns of interaction in teams that undermine learning. The patterns of defensiveness are often deeply engrained in how a team operates" (Senge, 1990, p. 10).

If we look at these points collectively, we can find, among them, a common key element—dialogue and freedom of expression. Without honest dialogue, how can we hold our ideas up for "rigorous scrutiny" so that we may be able to realize our assumptions and generalizations? Without dialogue, how can we build shared pictures of the future? The discipline of team learning also starts with dialogue.

In terms of dialogue, the problem in Chinese organizations is that people tend to shy away from it because leaders don't seem to enjoy honest dialogue. We have been quite strong in our economic reforms, but the necessity produced by the reforms for changes in non-economic arenas was adequately recognized. This is because reforms in many non-economic areas will necessarily cause greater demands for freedom of expression, which in turn may prove detrimental to the Communist Party's control of power and to the privileges enjoyed by those in power. Deng Xiaoping had called for political reform as early as 1980s, and party rule had been regularized and rationalized in the years since, but the essence of the party's monopoly on the economy and society has scarcely been touched. Ideological issues are so politically sensitive that reformers have been avoiding discussing them and have proceeded with reforms in the name of pragmatism and science. The leadership has little understanding of the rapid and vast moral and social changes underway in China (Hamrin, 1990). If they do, they purposely ignore these changes.

Why leaders do not welcome dialogue with freedom of expression concerns the question of power (Mumby, 1984). Dialogue with freedom of expression will surely expose inherent irrationalities in the current system of power. Our type of leadership is surely the transactional type instead of the transformational type as defined by Covey in his Principle-Centered Leadership. According to Covey, transactional leadership "is preoccupied with power and position, politics, and perks, focuses on tactical issues, and relies on human relations to lubricate human interactions" (p. 286). In many Chinese organizations, individual leaders set up new institutions and staff them with loyalists so that they can make freer use of resources within institutions under their control (Hamrin, 1990).

In 1986, Hu Yiaobang's campaign against official corruption at the highest level resulted in the arrest or imprisonment of a number of the offspring of high-level leaders. This galvanized opposition and undermined the campaign. What we need is to reform China's autocratic political culture through the development of scientific concepts and democratic values and institutions, of which dialogue and freedom of expression become the key elements (Hamrin, 1990). A study of Chinese Academy of Social Sciences found that more than 83% of China's urban dwellers believe that the country's bureaucracy is corrupt, and more than 63% of the cadres surveyed admitted that they were involved in corrupt practices (Salem, 1988). The question of public money is another big problem in Chinese organizations. Leaders waste public money in all possible ways; extravagant dinners and even exploitation of prostitution are among the prominent areas as journalistically reported. This problem concerning the public money results from governmental secrecy and mistrust between the people and the government. When people don't know how public money is used by the leaders and for what purposes, they tend to suspect that the leaders are using it in a corrupt way (Investigations are actually proving this suspicion). Leaders' abuse of public money only leads to employees' abuse of it. Dialogue will surely destroy this secrecy regarding leaders' use of public money, though dialogue will lead to trust. Theorists have spoken of popular alienation from the party and attacked bureaucratic privilege as the heart of China's problems.

Lack of dialogue is also reflected in the fact that "strategic decision-making about China's future remains dominated by the party elite and is constrained by the ideological and institutional imperatives necessary to retain that dominance" (Hamrin, 1990, pp. 210-211). The most obvious result is ad hoc reformism marked by sharp swings in policy that reflects reaction to the economic cycles inherent in a semi-planned economy. Dialogue will change this situation by allowing leaders to know what is happening in the people's minds and the economic reality and thus make policy-making pro-active rather than reactive.

Another cause of lack of dialogue in China is the Party's attitude toward true criticism. Periodically the Communist Party would encourage people to express their opinions. The biggest fiasco was the Hundred Flowers Campaign in 1956, during which everyone was urged to offer constructive criticism and comments about the shortcomings of the Communist Party. The following year all the people who had said anything were seized and punished. Most of the victims were educated intellectuals. After that there was almost complete silence in China, and all cultural activities stagnated. Such practice of encouraging and then suppressing criticism necessarily destroys any wish and courage for further expression.

A Discussion of Proposed Solutions to Problems in Chinese Organizations.

Free flow of information helps lead to trust and a more objective picture of reality. According to Moshar (1988), for China's economy to be efficient, information, capital, and goods must flow freely throughout the economic system. The Chinese Communist Party continues to insist on its myth of infallibility and repress criticism of its policy. Far too little reliable information, both of economic and non-economic variety, reaches Beijing for it to achieve economic growth without inflation, or successfully deregulate prices without causing further unemployment. In 1984, one of the primary authors of the Second China 2000 Study's summary volume produced a report of Chinese mega-trends. One mega-trend was "Simultaneous industrialization and broader, freer access to and use of information" (Hamrin, 1990, p. 124). Free flow of information decreases doubt, cynicism, complaints, and increases trust and understanding. Trust and understanding are what we urgently need now in China.

Freedom of speech and press instead of monologue by the Party. In China, self-expression can sometimes be self-destruction as expressed by Deetz (1992). Leaders really frown upon honest criticism. Communication between leaders and the people is mostly one-directional, in the form of a monologue and policies. We engage in the weekly "political study" only to listen to what our leaders have to tell us. Suggestions from the people are occasionally solicited but rarely implemented, which only discourages further suggestions and dialogue. Covey (1993) argued that true communication is a dialogue, not a monologue. Mutual understanding results in mutual influence. Yet it is very hard for the people to influence the leaders. Without a trustful relationship, people can become offending for a word. Many suffer imprisonment because of a brief comment. Communication is a matter of relationship, not one of words. It is far from enough to just publish the mission and values by the leadership. If people feel that the advocates of the mission and values are not living by these their own mission and values, the people will never believe in the mission and values.

Chinese government mostly fears public discussion lest it will create instability. Yet I'm sure that no government is forced to implement all the results from public discussion. Ignoring problems, on the other hand, is perfect preparation for another tumult, too many of which have plagued the New China in its short history of about 50 years. Chinese history after 1949 is a perfect pattern of short-term and abnormally quick development and then suddenly exploding ideological revolution. I really worry that another chaotic "revolution" may be in store for my country. The abnormally quick development is achieved by focusing our attention only on economy and by ignoring problems deeply inherent in the system. The sudden explosion of an ideological revolution also results from ignoring problems that have developed long enough.

To handle the social conflicts that emerge between people of different social status and to create a new society rich in information and creativity will require both a radical increase in freedom of expression on all levels and the growth of a new public morality that allows individual choice and expression while still encouraging social cooperation. Harrison (1994) argues that one of the most pressing needs in present organizations is for conflict strategies that provide opportunities "for free expression and dissent while minimizing deleterious psychological impacts on organizational members" (p. 270). So far, although Chinese leaders see a connection between development and democracy, the majority of these leaders view it through the lens of materialistic prosperity. The problem is that our political and economic systems inhibit the required mechanism for free expression to fuel steady development. China's best hope for moving to a new dynamic socialist order lies in creative reforms of the state structure to more rapidly create channels for the open competition of ideas, values, and power. Open societies, despite their complexities, achieve relative stability through competitive self-regulation and independence through interdependence. A nation cannot keep up in the post-industrial era without such political processes. In matters of policy, freedom of speech allows the most effective means in achieving given ends to have a better chance of getting adopted. Freedom of speech also provides a *check on leadership* that is corrupt, inefficient, and not complying with the legal system. Freedom of speech won't create an unstable society by encouraging agitation and possibly even violent change. Cross-national studies tend to show that more permissive societies also have the highest stability and degree of change in the long run through peaceful means. The explanation is partly that free speech provides a safety-valve which decreases the likelihood of resorting to violence.

A comprehensive rather than piecemeal fashion in approaching reforms. "Studies from *China Toward the Year 2000* showed that addressing interrelated problems in economic, social, scientific, and technical development must occur in a comprehensive rather than piecemeal fashion" (Hamrin, 1990, p, 49). To compete in this post-modern world, China needs, at a minimum, even more accurate strategic research and decision-making; realistic and anticipatory planning rather than manipulation of future goals as political promises and symbols of power; flexible and innovative decentralized economic entities that can respond quickly to the rapid changes in many characteristic of computerized economies; a means of increasing productivity not just in production but in the integrated process of production and services; a capable economic elite constantly upgrading managerial methods; a strong central financial control system that can fine-tune the economy to avoid serious fluctuations between inflation and recession; and, very importantly, a free intellectual environment conducive to scientific and humanistic advancement. But Chinese leaders and the broader elite have been slower to give equal attention to the political and cultural requirements of this technological competition, in large part because they are more difficult to address and such problems take much longer to alleviate. Yet repeated lessons from our brief history have irrefutably clinched that the easy way out is no way out.

Adjustment of the political system, an inseparable part of the economic reform. The resiliency of the market and the spontaneous emergence of thousands of small-scale enterprises that followed in the wake of the agricultural reforms caught China's leaders by surprise. According to Deng Xiaoping (1987, p. 189):

> ...If the Central Committee made any contribution in this respect, it was only by laying down the correct policy of invigorating the domestic economy. The fact that this policy has had such a favorable result shows that we made a good decision. But this result was not anything that I or any of the other comrades had foreseen; it just came out of the blue.

The lesson is simple: If government is limited to the enforcement of rational rules that do not interfere with private rights and production, then there is no need for a complex state planning apparatus and political cadre to monitor every move of the economic system. Individual self-interest will promote the nation's wealth, as Adam Smith envisioned, once the appropriate institutions are in place. Foremost among these institutions is a political system that guarantees freedom of expression and honest discussion. Thus a check and balance of power will be secured, the safest safety-valve to counterbalance the vicissitudes and fluctuations of the market forces.

In conclusion, the problems in Chinese organizations are actually also problems in many countries. What many leaders have in their minds are not the needs of the people, but the needs of a certain power group. Such leaders, however eloquent and logical in their arguments, cannot lead, because they are not "credible" (Kouzes & Posner, 1993). What we are having too much is a self-interest ethic, especially on the part of our leadership. What we are lacking too much is a service ethic, especially on the part of our leadership. Wherever and whenever the service ethic is adopted, problems lessen, leadership is simplified, and everybody's life becomes more joyful. Wherever and whenever the self-interest/competition ethic is adopted, we create more problems and dig deeper into our communal prison.

Leaders are people who are great in vision but humble in spirit. On the one hand, they are empowered with a super-ordinate purpose that transcends the cacophony of reality. On the other hand, leaders consider their power from vision as a tool to serve rather than an instrument for control. A discrepancy between what the leaders preach and what they practice will only confuse rather than direct and enlighten.

Notes:

1. The word "organization" in this article is interpreted in its broadest sense, including all levels of organizations. It can be as small as a small-size enterprise or as big as the whole nation.

2. Brief introductions to the Chinese leaders that appear in this article:

(1) Mao Zedong: Considered as the founding father of the New China, Mao Zedong led Chinese people through the pre-liberation revolutions and the post-liberation movements (economic or non-economic), including the disastrous Cultural Revolution. Mao died in 1976.

(2) Deng Xiaoping: Secretary General of the Communist party and member of the Politburo standing committee after the 1956 8th Party Congress and a chief victim of the Cultural Revolution. Deng was brought back to power by Mao in 1974 when it was learned that Premier Zhou Enlai was dying of cancer. Deng became paramount leader at the 1978 3rd Plenum after years of political struggle against Mao's close associates. Deng chose to give the top formal posts of party chief and premier to his protégés, but like Mao he retained control of the Central Military Commission, thus ensuring his unassailable preeminence. Deng died in 1997, just before the materialization of his dream, the return of Hong Kong.

(3) Hu Yaobang: Deng Xiaoping's chief lieutenant in the effort to demote Maoists and rehabilitate veteran officials in the late 1970s. Hu served variously as chief of the academy of science, the central party school, and the propaganda and organization departments in that period. He became the party's secretary-general in 1980 after the fall of Hua Guofeng. As a result of attacks by party and military conservatives and a falling out in 1986 with Deng over the issue of Deng's retirement and Hu's promotion, Hu was dismissed from office after admitting to serious mistakes in January 1989. Zhao Ziyang replaced him. Hu died in April 1989, which triggered the historic student movement that year.

(4) Zhao Ziyang: Born 1919, present position—disgraced, and under house arrest. Zhao Ziyang pioneered bold economic reform in China but was dragged down in a crisis sparked by popular demands for parallel political freedoms. At one time considered heir-apparent to Deng Xiaoping, Zhao became Communist Party leader in November 1987 at the party's 13th congress, when many veteran revolutionaries retired from top posts. Barely 18

months later, those same old men, fearful of the social changes Zhao's reforms had triggered, re-emerged to back hard-liners demanding his overthrow. During the 1989 student-led protests around Tiananmen Square, Zhao, with tears in his eyes, beseeched student leaders to end the demonstrations that were subsequently crushed by the military. Zhao's supporters on September 10, 1997 issued a daring call for his release, saying that restricting his rights and freedoms for eight years is "abnormal."

Bibliography

Cheng, N. (1988). Life and death in Shanghai. New York: Penguin Books.

Covey, S. R. (1993). Spiritual roots of human relations. Salt Lake City, UT: Deseret Book Company.

Deetz, S. (1992). Democracy in an age of corporate colonization. Albany: State University of New York Press.

Deming, W.E. (1986). Out of the crisis. Cambridge, MA: Massachusetts Institute of Technology, Center for Advanced Engineering Study.

Deng, Xiaoping. (1987). Fundamental Issues in Present-Day China. Translated by the Bureau for the Compilation and Translation of Works of Marx, Engels, Lenin, and Stalin under the Central Committee of the Communist Party of China. Beijing: Foreign Languages Press.

Deming, W.E. (1993). The new economics. Cambridge, MA: Massachusetts Institute of Technology, Center for Advanced Engineering Study.

Dorn, A.J. & Wang, X. (1990). Economic reform in China: Problems and prospects. Chicago: The University of Chicago Press.

Dutt, G. (1967). Rural communes of China: Organizational problems. New York: Asia Publishing House.

Faure, E. (1958). The serpent and the tortoise: Problems of the New China. Trans. L. F. Edwards. New York: St. Martin's Press.

Hamrin, C. L. (1990). China and the challenge of the future: Changing political patterns. Boulder, CO: Westview Press.

Hayes, R. H., Wheelright, S. C., & Clark, K. B. (1988). Dynamic manufacturing: Creating the learning organization. New York: The Free P.

Hesselbein, F., Goldsmith, M. & Beckhard, R. (Eds.) (1996). The leader of the future. San Francisco: Jossey-Bass.

Isaacs, W.N. (1993). Taking flight: Dialogue, collective thinking and organizational learning. Organizational Dynamics, 22, 24-39.

Kilman, R. H., Kilman, I., & associates. (1994). Managing ego energy: The transformation of personal meaning into organizational success. San Francisco: Jossey-Bass.

Kimberly, J. R., & Miles, R. H. (1980). The organizational life cycle: Issues in the creation, transformation, and decline of organizations. San Francisco: Jossey-Bass.

Kouzes, J. M. & Posner, B. Z. (1993). Credibility: How leaders gain and lose it, why people demand it. San Francisco: Jossey-Bass.

Levy, A., & Merry, U. (1986). Organizational transformation: Approaches, strategies, theories. New York: Praeger.

Michael, S., & Scott, M. (Eds.). (1991). The corporation of the 1990s: Information technology and organizational transformation. New York: Praeger.

Moshar, S. (1988). China's economic puzzle. Wall Street Journal, 8, 19.

Mumby, D.K. (1984). Ideology and power in organization. Unpublished doctoral dissertation, Southern Illinois University.

Nadler, D. A., Shaw, R. B., Walton, A. E. & associates. (1995). Achieving successful organizational transformation. San Francisco: Jossey-Bass.

Nadler, L., & Nadler, Z. (1994). Strategic readiness: The making of the learning organization. San Francisco: Jossey-Bass.

Peck, M.S. (1978). The road less traveled. New York: Simon and Schuster.

Persico, J. (Ed.). (1992). The TQM transformation: A model for organizational change. White Plains, NY: Quality Resources.

Raffini, J. P. (1993). Winners without losers. Needham Heights, MA: Allyan and Bacon.

Salem, E. (1988). Fighting sticky fingers: Corrupt cadres erode support for economic reforms. Far Eastern Economic Review, June 16.

Schein, E.H. (1993). On dialogue, culture and organizational learning. Organizational Dynamics, 22, 40-51.

Senge, P. M. (1990). The fifth discipline. New York: Doubleday.

Southerland, D. (1988). China plans to sell stock in state-owned enterprises. Washington Post, 21 September, F1 & F5.

Whitsett, D. A., & Burling, I. R. (1996). Achieving successful organizational transformation. Westport, CT: Quorum Books.

Xue, M. (1982). Current economic problems in China. Ed. and Trans. K. K. Fung. Boulder, CO: Westview Press.

3

Uncensored Web Publications and Chinese Democracy

I remember one Chinese philosopher said that all Chinese people speak with but one mind. The basis for our perception is what is given to us by the government-controlled mass media. This is perhaps why nationwide chaotic upheavals (e.g., the "Big Leap Forward" Movement and the "Cultural Revolution") are not so difficult to occur in my country. We have more than 1 billion people in China; it is a great pity that we have only one mind, if the philosopher is correct.

After my arrival in the U.S., I found some inspirational Chinese electronic magazines on the Internet. They are sponsored by volunteer Chinese students and scholars in the U.S. and are uncensored by the government. Through these magazines I see different pictures of our history, government and culture. Contributors are open to discuss problems concerning the country. Interestingly many contributors strongly support continued power for our supposedly corrupt government. If our government sees all this through the Internet, I suppose they won't fear dissidents so much as they do now; they will be more willing to go further on the road of democracy. Our government should learn this lesson from publications on the Internet: Open and democratic communication won't necessarily cause the overthrow of the government (unless it is irremediably corrupt); open communication won't cause chaos in that it is a system of balance and check. Uncensored publications on the Internet are obviously teaching us this lesson.

0-595-28517-1